Dreams of the Immortal City Savannah

By Aberjhani

ALSO BY ABERJHANI

I Made My Boy Out of Poetry (1998)

The Wisdom of W.E.B. Du Bois (2003/2017)

Encyclopedia of the Harlem Renaissance (2003/2010)

Christmas When Music Almost Killed the World (2007)

The American Poet Who Went Home Again (2008)

ELEMENTAL, The Power of Illuminated Love (2008)

The River of Winged Dreams (2010)

Savannah: The Immortal City (Editor, 2010)

Savannah: Brokers, Bankers, and Bay Lane, Inside the Slave Trade (Editor, 2011)

Visions of a Skylark Dressed in Black (2012)

In memory of: Vanda Clark Trappio Patton and Dr. Abigail Jordan, two icons of the civil and human rights movements.

And for Carrie L. Collins, whose enthusiastic reading of stories from the *Dreams* manuscript provided motivation and determination to keep striving for the finish line.

"It is true that a person always remains a person and utterly separate and apart from every other person. But it is equally true that each person is destined to reach with others an understanding and a unity which transcend individuality…"

–Thomas Merton (*A Life in Letters*)

"On our temperate side we have a series of songs in us, guarding us, wings of communication between our calm breath and our highest fevers..."

—Rene Char (*Put on Guard*)

Acknowledgments

This book exists only partly because I could not abandon the idea of working on it throughout the past decade, even though there was no funding made available to ensure its completion and a succession of severe weather events and other survival-issues strongly challenged the likelihood it would ever see the light of day. While funding was not made available for the title itself, I did become the blessed recipient of a PEN American Center Writers' Fund Grant at a time when it had become questionable I would be able continue working on anything at all. The organization has recognized and championed the efforts of many writers working under different forms of oppression around the world, so I am profoundly grateful for its intervention at an extremely vulnerable time in my life.

It is also my honor to recognize those who have made their life stories part of mine in such a way that at times the journey of the one became almost indistinguishable from that of the other. By allowing the currents of our extended narratives to periodically cross and merge in unique authentic ways, they have contributed greatly to the pages that follow and therefore earned their places in them. A few of their names have been changed out of respect for their privacy and in such instances the abbreviation NCP, for Name Changed to Protect Privacy, will appear in parentheses (NCP) beside them. Among those whose encouragement and various forms of support made *Dreams of the Immortal City Savannah* possible are, in no particular order: Dr. William White, Velma Washington, Barry Sheehy, Dr. Patricia Stewart, Nilton Silva, Veranda Ferreira, the late Dr. Ja A. Jahannes, Benjamin Bacon, and Dessie Baker.

For their assistance with research and/or for making available specific resources, I thank: the staff of Savannah's W.W. Law Center

Library, the staff of the Carnegie Branch Library (please see appendix C), and that of the Bull Street Library Genealogy and History Room. I am also, as I have been in the past, grateful to members of the Telfair Museum of Art, specifically Beth Moore and Harry DeLorme, for sharing their expert knowledge on the museum's acquisitions and exhibits. Likewise, my thanks to the Chatham Area Transit office's Valerie Ragland for her shared insights on the organization's history.

And last, but nowhere near least, I am grateful to poet Carol Phelan Aebby for bringing to my attention the excellent work of the literary visionaries at Cyberwit.net, and to those same visionaries for the time, energy, and resources devoted to placing *Dreams of the Immortal City Savannah* into the hands of readers around the world.

For any whose names should have been included but were unintentionally omitted, please forgive me. I am truly grateful for any and all contributions to this work.

Aberjhani

Introduction

Cities are as much composites of human memories, desires, and personalities as they are constructions of steel, concrete, glass, roaring energy, and ever-expanding technologies. Stitched together like the patches of romantic fantasies and terrifying night terrors that give Hollywood and Bollywood some of their most successful creations, diverse experiences combine to create private narratives often linked to public concerns. These observations, as demonstrated by the stories in this volume, hold as mesmerizingly true for Savannah, Georgia, as for any other locale. They embrace the challenges of here-and-now at the same time that they honor the courageous endeavors of yesterday.

Credit for the original conception of Savannah as a poetically-proclaimed Immortal City should probably go to the state of Georgia's founder, James Edward Oglethorpe, who in 1733 hoped to see the entire new colony become a shining example of enlightenment in progressive action. The actual term was later put to exceptionally good use by historian Barry Sheehy in his work documenting Savannah's role as a major center of slave-trading right up until the American Civil War. Any enduring applicability of such a courageous notion would have to be attributed to its ever-evolving diverse citizenry and the predispositions of history itself.

Savannah's designation in 2018 as the fastest growing city in Georgia and its increasing importance on national and international levels are steadily reversing the social dynamics that once led natives to label it with the comical names "Slow-vannah" and "Save-Anna." Temptation to dub it SCAD-vannah, in reference to the Savannah College of Art and Design's irrefutable impact, is hard to avoid considering the famous art school's ubiquitous presence throughout and beyond the region.

In the impressive city design generally attributed to Oglethorpe, the founder's vision went far beyond any idea of picturesque squares which might one day entice rovers from across the globe to spend time in the city, thus giving natives and transplants reasons to lay claim to measures of justifiable pride. It was a way for colonists to simultaneously structure, empower, and extend communities. You could call it his dream for the future of populations that would eventually grow diverse in ways for which he could hardly have fully prepared himself or anyone else. One of his most interesting proposals was this:

"Each Family should have a Farm in the Country and an Alotment sufficient for a House and a Garden in the Town." (Oglethorpe, James. *Some Account of the Design of the Trustees for Establishing Colonys in America*, Univ. of GA, p. 37, 1990)

What might the application of such an enlightened social experiment look like in this second decade of the 21st century? It certainly dared to propose more for individual citizens than the 2017 strategic plan adopted by city administrators to secure a Triple A bond rating by the year 2030. It also went considerably further than the brilliant options proposed in 2018 by the informed strategists affiliated with the Congress for New Urbanism. With the eradication of areas once referred to as Commons and the aggressive often predatory acquisition of properties in general, Oglethorpe's suggestion would be an impossible undertaking. There are those who loudly proclaim the quest for Triple A status the same. But the theoretical impact of such concepts––as in the effects they could possibly have on the higher-than-national-average percentage of children living in poverty in the state as well as those living far from it—makes for some staggering worthwhile considerations if not practical solutions.

In his dream of Georgia and its future, Oglethorpe took into account nearly every conceivable environmental and developmental factor as it existed at the time and as it might come to exist generations down the road. The psychological dispositions of disabled settlers, how colonists and the mother country of England would financially enrich each other, and the role which the institution of marriage would play in the colony's ultimate success or failure were serious definitive factors. What he did not, and perhaps could not, envision was the extent to which increasing cultural diversity and individual genius would begin to alter our collective experience of history—like a singular flood of epic dimensions, or the strike of a powerful meteor the size of Ohio, completely rearranging a once-familiar landscape. His wise cordial diplomacy toward Yamacraw chief Tomochichi and the initial decision to prohibit slavery in the colony (though yes, he did indeed import slave labor for a time from neighboring South Carolina) indicated he understood well enough it would have some meaningful impact. How much of one remained a question only time could one day answer.

The focus of his mission was to secure a resource-rich outpost that would benefit England to the tune of a profit of £6,700 from the financed immigration of 125 families. In this, it may be said contemporary city leaders—given many modern advantages— have the better stated proposal as they move to link municipal jobs and functions to specific outcomes in the areas of: public safety, infrastructure, neighborhood revitalization, increased economic strength, and poverty reduction. These variables, of course, could only exist after the sluggish passage of time but the option to exercise foresight is always pinned to the moment at hand.

Almost 300 years after a succession of wars, hurricanes, plagues, fires, migrations, and the *Emancipation Proclamation*, Oglethorpe's original basic physical design of the colony has proven enduring even while the city as a whole has morphed into a cosmopolitan center of commerce, diverse demographics, cultural arts, military facilities, and scientific research dedicated to preserving the surrounding natural environment as well as further developing means to leave earth's boundaries altogether. Consequently, if he were able to see his masterful cityscape as it stands now, the founder might very well, as some have suggested, recognize it based on his plan. But he would also have to make some serious adjustments in regard to how society itself has evolved and, as framed by his enlightened disposition, might or might not be pleased by what he discovered.

The relative independence of women and adult children from their male sponsors could strike him as a good thing likely to strengthen the practice of democracy and social civility in general. Undoubtedly the abundance of educational facilities in the area—Armstrong State/Georgia Southern University, Savannah State University, Savannah College of Art and Design (SCAD), Georgia Institute of Technology, and South University among others—would earn approval. The presence in influential positions of "effeminate types" that he considered undesirable as settlers of the colony would require some re-thinking and maybe prompt him to seek briefing or counsel from various authority figures. The preponderance of beautiful churches dotting the landscape—given the Enlightenment period's lean toward secularism—not to mention a highly-visible mosque and Jewish presence would inspire deep reflection as well. Who, we might wonder, would be willing to explain why prisons in Georgia and the rest of America still represent some of the most overt forms of political, class, and racial oppression known to humanity, especially (at the time of this writing) given the sadly disproportionate population of the country to the world's population of prison inmates?

Moreover: imagine the expression on his face upon discovering descendants of African slaves, whom he once cautioned would violently rebel against enslavement and destroy the colonial enterprise if slavery was made legal, eventually came to comprise the majority of his colony's first city's population. In addition, they became over time some of its chief builders—as educators, laborers, ministers, farmers, journalists, business people, and, eventually, as mayors.

The story of people of African descent in Savannah has been one of steady progression marred by the kind of political, economic, and social setbacks which have impacted African-American communities throughout the United States since the days of the Old Jim Crow leading up to the New Jim Crow. Yet it may be argued that in some ways the losses have been more severely felt in Savannah because of the black community's status as the oldest of its kind in Georgia.

From Oglethorpe's temporary use of slaves imported from South Carolina to clear land for the new colony, and the later importation of Africans from Africa itself during the Atlantic Slave trade to the establishment of Savannah State University (originally the Georgia State Industrial College for Colored Youth) in 1890, and, the successive election of three black mayors from 1996 until 2016, the community has steadily evolved. It has also seen many of its most talented individuals move away and stay away due to seemingly insurmountable blocks to their hopes for upward mobility within their beloved hometown as well as other factors considered sad, deadly, or tragic. Consider, for example, what happened in 2015: following one of numerous gang incidents to occur in a black neighborhood, a group of concerned citizens took to the streets in a march against violence. Interviewing one of the gang members who acknowledged participating in such destructiveness, a TV reporter asked how it made him feel to see the people of his community publicly mourning the lives of individuals lost to the chaos. With his face and voice obscured to ensure the safety of his three-year-old daughter, the young man gave a very unexpected answer:

"I mean, you know, they should'a been out here marchin' an' doin' somethin' long before now. Everybody get upset and got somethin' to say when somebody they know get shot, but what about all the other times when it's just us?" He added that, for the sake of his daughter, he wanted to get away from gang life but believed it might be an inherited trait. "My daddy was in a gang and his daddy was in one before him. They both got shot by bangers."

It was a blood-chilling way of saying: This is all I know, all I have ever been, and all I really expect to be until death sends a bullet for me also. If Oglethorpe's dream-plans were designed to provide a better scenario for him, he certainly did not know about it and likely would not have placed much faith in them if he did. But why such an unyielding mindset in a town where so many residents, as well as potential transplants, have been eyeing enviable indicators of steady economic growth surpassing the state's and that of many other cities? Why do such indicators typically seem to mean little or nothing at all to segments of the population whose lives and succeeding generations are consistently hemmed in by poverty, inadequate education, racial disparities, and imprisonment? Why did Oglethorpe's vision, or for that matter Martin Luther King Jr.'s dream, seem to hold no meaning whatsoever for him?

The stories in *Dreams of the Immortal City Savannah* do not focus directly on the unusual racial dynamics which have influenced the city's growth and development, or lack thereof, since the days of Oglethorpe and slavery. Unfolding on levels ranging from the private and familial to the public and institutional, they offer examinations of what happens when dreams, visions, and nightmares converge, or clash, within the context of a given life impacted by cultural geographies merging within regions of a creative mind. Oglethorpe would have known something about that. In "Cities of Lights and Shadows and Prayers," a writer moves back and forth between awareness of himself in 1990s Savannah and a false memory of interactions with cultural icons in 1940s Paris. "A Brazilian Thanksgiving in Georgia" examines the paradox of an estranged caregiver rediscovering the meanings of family and fate through a surprise holiday visit from Brazilian immigrants. "Trees Down Everywhere" documents attempts to prevent the flooding of a civil rights icon's historic Victorian home during the ravages of 2016 Hurricane Matthew and at a controversial moment in Donald Trump's campaign for the U.S. presidency. The title story, "Dreams of the Immortal City," confronts the legacy of slavery while the closing narratives examine modern conditions and hopes for the future.

"The Bridge and the Monument: A Tale of Two Legacies" was first published in *The American Poet Who Went Home Again*. The updated text included in this volume is presented in tribute to Dr. Abigail Jordan, whose passing (January 9, 2019) was reported just as edits were undergoing completion. It is also included because of the role it has come to play in ongoing present-day efforts to change the current name of the bridge spanning the Savannah River from the city's downtown area to Hutchinson Island.

Whether in the instance of the great Oglethorpe establishing America's thirteenth colony, modern-day residents negotiating the wisdom of fleeing the wrath of hurricanes, or contemporary African-Americans acclimating themselves to the reality that with black power for black people comes black responsibility for diverse populations, history makes one demand upon us all. It demands we adapt to the ragged flow of its ever-changing trends and reconfigurations. The only alternative is to await one's own demise. Better, perhaps, as the stories which follow suggest, to step back long enough to reevaluate the kinds of assumptions, practices, and behaviors which too often encourage disruptive conflicts or personal defeats, and then try taking a more enlightened, more empowered, step forward.

Aberjhani
Savannah, GA
Feb 2019 Harlem Renaissance Centennial

Contents

Black and white art detail from *City of Lights-Kaleidoscope Moon for Children Gone Too Soon #6* by Aberjhani.

Cities of Lights and Shadows and Dreams

"As people who had the life of Savannah firmly stamped upon their minds, Aiken and O'Connor had absorbed the urbanity of a small city that, when they were young there, still drew cultural power from London and Paris. But the two suffered wounds of the soul there, Aiken more than O'Connor." —Ted R. Spivey (*Flannery O'Connor: the Woman, the Thinker, the Visionary*)

For years I had told friends and myself that my one favorite city was Paris, France. This exalted preference had been intensified by a very strange memory–as false as a five-dollar bill with a grinning emoji plastered where Abraham Lincoln's noble beard should be–which for a long time repeatedly surfaced and insisted it was real.

The memory was of a cool day early in May 1946. Much of the talk in Paris was about the fact that Richard Wright, the famous author of *Native Son* and *Black Boy,* who had been becoming very vocal about his needs for greater intellectual freedom and political flexibility, would soon arrive in the city of lights with his wife Ellen and daughter Julia for the first time.

To prove just how false this persistent memory was, in 1946 I had not even been "a glimmer in my father's eye," as the saying went back then, and at least another decade would pass before I would become such. Nevertheless, I imagined myself one of those African-American soldiers who had remained in France after World War II and explored ways to make a life for myself there, taking advantage of the new G.I. Bill to go to school, and set up a small jazz supper club called The Hot Fried Piano.

At The Hot Fried Piano, the great international diva Josephine Baker might drop in to enjoy her native "soul food" when she felt like it and maybe pay for her supper by enchanting customers with a song or a smile. Afterwards, I would step up to the mic and recite my own brand of negritude surrealist poetry. The Hot Fried Piano, it seemed, was somewhere in the Latin Quarter and attracted just enough clientele to keep the music going and the menu half-full.

II.

The main problem with the club was every now and then I entered a room and did not see any of the expected patrons. Instead of preparing for their next set, the musicians were talking and laughing, then sometimes playing when the mood struck them. No one passionately debated existentialism in French, and I could not taste the aromas of wine, fresh bread, or savory stew mingling in the air. What I saw in those moments was me in a different more recent 1990s time in another city, Savannah, Georgia, standing in a space on the second floor of a three-story structure known as The Blue House.

In this place a small crowd of artists, poets, musicians, soldiers, and social theorists had gathered to share their talents and talk about possibilities for Savannah's future. They were black, white, Latino, male, female, heterosexual, LGBT, some native to the city and some transplants, veterans of war, and advocates for peace. Periodically during these gatherings, I would hold up a copy of either Tyler Stovall's travel essay, *Paris Noir*, or Kay Boyle's and Robert McAlmon's classic memoir, *Being Geniuses Together,* to emphasize a point. Shared creativity, I suggested, sometimes evolved into important cultural arts movements and a strong sense of community among creative individuals who in turn made important contributions to society and history. Then one evening I walked into this Blue House room in Savannah where my friends' faces were shining like Christmas presents and calmly announced: I am moving to Paris.

"That's where you belong," responds one. "Like Baldwin and Eugene Jacques Bullard did."

"Like Dexter Gordon in that movie *'Round Midnight'*!" says another.

"Didn't he have some hardcore personal drug issues in that film?"

"Here's to Paris!"

"Yeah man, here's to Paris!"

At first it was too frightening to question the difference between what I saw in the room filled with people from the Blue House and what I experienced so clearly in an uncertain memory. Sooner or later I would have to accept that their knife-sharp distinctions meant that one was likely more true, more real, than the other. But for a time, I persisted in the memory of anticipating the arrival of Richard Wright in Paris.

It happened when he entered by train on the 8th of May and it was my intention to help him make his way through the crowds at the Gare Saint-Lazare station to a waiting taxi. It turned out, however, that the reigning queen of North American expatriates in Europe, author Gertrude Stein, had already arranged for Douglas Schneider of the American Embassy to meet the great author and take him back to the Trianon-Palace Hotel in a first-class limousine. Fortunately for me, the hotel was also in the Latin Quarter so I was able to ride along and enjoy the look of thrilled satisfaction on Wright's face as the limousine rolled through the city down the wide avenue of the Champs Elysees, went gliding through the Place de la Concorde past the culture-stuffed Louvre and along the Left Bank where new schools of philosophy were born and argued on the lips of passionate souls every ten minutes.

I became more than a little excited when I heard him say, just as Douglas Schneider recorded in *Souvenir de Richard Wright*, "I had no idea that one city could contain in so little space so many treasures, so many flowers, so many grey stones, all beautiful...so very beautiful." (Those words were not completely inapplicable to Savannah, especially when talking about River Street or other areas in the Historic District.)

In the days and nights that follow, his time is absorbed by a series of receptions: he meets his champion Gertrude Stein, in whose work he has discovered such eerie connections to his own; he greets the legendary Sylvia Beach of Shakespeare and Company Bookstore fame, the woman whose patronage helped make the literary legacies of James Joyce and Ernest Hemingway a celebrated reality. The publisher Gaston Gallimard and literary titans Simone de Beauvoir and Jean Paul Sartre, and many others all come to lend encouragement and empowerment as he considers permanently relocating—as in exiling himself—to Paris. Wright's presence in the city seems somehow to make it less important that times are difficult economically, that electrical power gets turned off for several hours every day, or that food is rationed and gas often not available at all. He is like a black flame come to intensify the spark of hope for cultural rebirth and spiritual renewal after the long suffocating nightmare of Nazi occupation that humbled and terrorized the city.

III.

As the excitement over the celebrity author grew stronger each day I was able to gradually decrease instances of walking through doors in The Hot Fried Piano and finding myself in The Blue House. The very last time this occurred I saw myself standing in the center of the room holding several sheets of paper while reciting poetry from them. Once I completed the last of three poems, people politely applauded and snapped their fingers. A young woman with earth-brown skin and classic African beauty walked up to me, looked directly into my eyes and said, "Man you got all kinds 'a power in your poetry. Why you holdin' it back?"

She was known to me as India and one day in an unforeseen future I would be at a holiday gathering with family members when someone would turn on the television and I would gasp to watch another woman named Oprah Winfrey introduce her to the world as India Arie. For the moment before that one in the future, I was as stunned by, as I was grateful for, her boldness.

"What makes you think I'm holding back?"

"I can feel it and I can hear it. I've seen you at the Gallery Espresso open mic and sometimes you cut loose cause you know you got a lot to say and people need to hear it. Then other times you step back like you gon' hurt somebody feelings but you can't be doing that. Because, and I don't mean to sound offensive or nothing—"

"Because it weakens me and cheats them of a chance to deal with the words on their own terms."

"See there, you knew what I was talking about all along."

She then lifted her acoustic guitar and moved gracefully into the spot I had just left.

When these scenes from The Blue House faded altogether I began to feel safer though not always happier because I also started to understand how much I cared about the people behind the door and to realize we were, all of us, doing something important. They were not part of the traumas of the past, they were something healing and new. That did not matter, I told myself, I was in Paris and the city of lights was where I would stay. Then late one night after closing The Hot Fried Piano I sat down to record sales figures in an accounting ledger— but instead of doing that I wrote the following:

It becomes increasingly clear to me that I've been experiencing some cognitive static and imbalance because I'm still physically living in one environment when I've already mentally and spiritually projected myself into a different future or past environment. Remaining in Savannah is something I simply cannot see, yet thus far I have not obtained the means to move elsewhere. Has any other period in my life anywhere else on this planet ever been more like living in the Twilight Zone than right now? Everything is either forthcoming, or in the past, with nothing of any tangible substance in the present. It's an awkward, vulnerable, and often painful place to be where one feels like a character in a Kafka or Borges story searching carefully through layers of smoke and illusion for some semblance of sanity or reason.

Staring at the words written across columns intended for numbers, a gentle understanding began to push insistently against me. The uncertain moments and questionable places in which we find ourselves are just as likely to choose us as we are to elect them and when that happens we must either agree with fate's unknown purposes or accept the risk of destruction that comes with battling against them. What I had come to call a memory, I finally understood, was not one at all—it was a battlefield in the form of a dream. Knowing that, however, did not make it any easier to do what I knew I must and I continued my French sojourn with altered intentions.

IV.

Although not of the league of the literary elite, I was one of those onyx-skinned children of humanity about whom Wright had written extensively in his fiction, memoirs, and essays, and this allowed us to greet each other with genuine enthusiasm when we ran into one another on the boulevard or when he dropped by The Hot Fried Piano for a taste of the United States. Then it so happened one afternoon that while taking a break, I was enjoying a table alone at a sidewalk café on the Left Bank when I looked up to see him crossing the street, moving towards me like a spaceman dazed by a recent fall to earth. The hat pulled down to his brow and the scarf around his neck and chin made it appear almost as if he was trying to disguise himself. Therefore, I did not say anything when he walked past me and went inside the café. Then he stepped back out a minute later with a bottle of water in his hand, sat down across from me, and said, "Hey man."

I manage not to choke on my coffee or drop the cup. He tells me that in some of my poetry he detects strong journalistic tendencies which will later serve me well as I begin to write in other genres. He adds that he has also heard heavy allusions to magic which could make poetry dangerous.

"But when," I ask, "is the last time anything or anyone has been 'safe' in this terrified world of ours?"

For some reason this makes him laugh louder than I have ever heard him laugh before.

"She's been a wonderful hostess and haven, hasn't she?" he asks, looking out toward the broad slow flow of the Seine River and letting his eyes swallow the light bouncing off its surface.

He glances sideways to see if I understood everything he meant by the question and I am astonished when I realize I do understand. He is not speaking merely about the relief from racial tensions and the pleasure of celebrated cultural diversity we have been able to enjoy as individuals. He is speaking of the many black American writers and artists and educators, men and women, who came to Paris before us and because of it were able to slow their panicked breathing long enough to discover and preserve their voices as committed creative artists and social activists. Having come here to fulfill a private agenda, we have also extended a noble historic tradition of mutual cultural exchange and enrichment.

Whereas the writer Victor Sejour had been born a free black man in the United States during the early 1800s, it took the move to France for him to gain an education and evolve into a celebrated playwright and novelist. The painter Henry Ossawa Tanner, educator Anna Julia Cooper, author Jean Toomer, author Langston Hughes, sculptress Meta Vaux Warrick Fuller and scores of others made the journey just to hear themselves think as singular individuals without the skull-cracking roar of racial oppression defining every impression or perception. Simply by allowing its darker-hued brothers and sisters to openly discuss ideas without having to constantly justify, defend, or survive the color of their skin, whether in classrooms of the great Sorbonne or while walking un-hunted down a boulevard, Paris made a crucial contribution to what would become known as the Harlem Renaissance and to the legacy of African-American intellectual traditions in general. An actual community of American Blacks had formed in the city just after World War I and, fluctuating population figures notwithstanding, have been there ever since.

"Genius will do whatever it must to survive, won't it?" I ask without really expecting an answer.

He smiles and is about to respond when a well-dressed man with an equally well-dressed woman beside him approaches us and says loudly, "Oh, there you are, but monsieur Richard we are late for your lecture and must now hurry. Hurry, hurry, hurry!"

After that moment, the memory grows fuzzy: I suspect because the more responsible side of my mind insists that I acknowledge this is much more of an oddly real-time kind of dream than a memory. The inner-confession makes me laugh out loud and silently wonder because there are other cities–London, New York, Philadelphia, San Francisco, and Berlin among them–where I actually have sat down and enjoyed moving conversations with inspiring writers. How Paris had come to cast such a powerful spell of desire and nostalgia from thousands of miles away remains an enigma. I'm thinking it may have something to do with the magic which Wright said could make poetry dangerous.

V.

It was, in fact, in Savannah decades later while fully awake in 2003 that I attended a book signing at Chef Joe Randall's cooking school and there met an African-American woman, Dr. Monique Y. Wells, who actually had been living in France for quite some time. Operating there a successful tourism company specializing in sites associated with black history, she was back in America promoting her cookbook, *Food for the Soul: A Texas Expatriate Nurtures Her Culinary Roots in Paris,* and, for her husband and friends still abroad, shopping for items not easily found in Europe. For someone such as I, who had made the choice to serve the needs of others rather than indulge personal desires to travel and write abroad, she might easily have been Josephine Baker herself, or the legendary nightclub hostess Bricktop, or the amazing cabaret singer Florence Mills, all of Harlem Renaissance fame. Getting an autographed copy of the cookbook gave me an opportunity to tell her I had co-authored an encyclopedia on the jazz-age renaissance which would be published later that year. She was surprised to receive such news in Savannah and said she hoped we could talk about it before leaving the city.

Two days later as she was preparing to begin her journey back across the Atlantic, Dr. Wells called and invited me to join her for coffee downtown at Starbucks on Broughton Street, a block north of Wright Square. A brief intense storm rolled through before we got there and once seated at a sidewalk table beneath an awning I told her the climate in Savannah was semi-tropical and we had entered the semi-monsoon season. The rain-slicked streets, freshly-washed storefronts, steaming bodies of passers-by, and air still humid from the mini-storm created an image perfect for an artist with the sensibilities of a Vincent Van Gogh or a Leonid Afremov. Already the sun was coming out again and its subdued radiance cloaked everything with a shimmer of antique gold. Someone should be painting this right now, I thought, then steered my attention back in the direction of my new friend.

The languidness of her wise brown eyes, for whatever odd reason, reminded me of Michel Proust's and for a second I had to resist imagining we were elsewhere. It was important to recognize the moment was unfolding on a street where as a child I used to walk with my gaze fixed on the sidewalk pavement to avoid the unwelcoming glances of Whites. It was important to acknowledge that just a century and a half ago Black People like us were sold at regularly-scheduled auctions in the square just behind us. Just a few blocks west of where we were sitting, it was important to recall, I had gotten my first job cleaning up the old Allied Department Store. It was there, while scrubbing toilets, washing windows, and mopping floors, I managed to save enough money to buy my first typewriter and began studying theories on how certain people managed to transform seemingly cursed lives into gorgeously fulfilled destinies.

Spread out on the table beside our cups of coffee (for me) and tea (for her) were *Encyclopedia of the Harlem Renaissance* page galleys, and among these a long article on Paris that gave us much more to discuss than we otherwise might have been inclined to because she had, obviously, been living manifestations of this passion to a far greater more tangible degree than I. When asked about the size of the African-American community there, she surprised me by answering it no longer numbered in the thousands as reportedly it once did; the figure was now closer to two or three hundred. My answers to her questions about life in Savannah made her laugh as I shared stories of how the unprecedented success of *Midnight in the Garden of Good and Evil* had apparently caused a temporary collective loss of sanity in the city. For two hours it seemed whatever had driven me to construct a false memory of being in France neither existed nor mattered. As our visit came to an end, I felt like a portal to another existence, to a part of my life I had finally gotten to live for just a few minutes, was closing.

If the Paris of my imagination had been a city and a time spilling over with promises of light upon light, what did that make the Savannah of my autobiographical reality? Was it necessarily a place suffused, for me, with nothing more than shadows of enigma and regret? When allowing illumination to seep into those shadows I could see reasons why something in me might pretend to run away. Or escape: there I was at three or four years old running with outstretched arms to embrace someone I loved and then, suddenly, found myself knocked flat on my back because I was wearing the same pajamas I had worn to bed the night before. There I was again a couple of years later feeling the fire of scalding water melt the skin from my right arm and not too long after that horror obeying the school teacher who instructed me to stand in front of the class and tell everyone how my adolescent brother Robert Lee had been shot in the back by a policeman. Further years down the calendar after I'd just turned twelve or thirteen a would-be rapist decided I was someone he had to have and I disagreed forcefully enough to almost break his neck before he successfully cracked my skull with a broken piece of concrete and, afraid that I was dead, ran off down deserted railroad tracks.

Days and nights of sadistic hunger, years of watching one dream after another deferred for no acceptably explicable reason, growing up to leave and return and find so little had changed for far too many could all easily swell into a mass of memories heaped into terrorizing shadows. The next-to-final question would have to be should I or anyone allow them to define the higher qualities of hope, mercy, or love in life? The answer could be as healing and liberating as it might be fatal or damning.

Study detail from *Flowers and Wings for Her Tears and Years* by Aberjhani.

A Brazilian Thanksgiving in Savannah

"...Love has no awareness of merit or de-merit; it has no scale by which its portion may be weighed or measured. It does not seek to balance giving and receiving. Love loves; this is its nature."

—Howard Thurman (*A Strange Freedom*)

The brutal images from the history of slavery in North America are fairly well-known and if they were not so cruel they could almost be referred to as stereotypical: women and men lashed with whips until flesh hung like rags from their bodies, women and men raped whenever an owner or privileged individual felt the urge, and members of families sold away from each other (as during the 1859 "Weeping Time" auction in Savannah) whenever it suited an owner's economic discretion. One of the more inhumane and haunting images of the institution, although rarely presented in books or on film, is one that actually transcends slavery itself and to this day challenges societies all over the world. As related by such heroines and heroes of American history as Harriet Tubman and Frederick Douglass, it is the image what often happened to slaves who had already outlived what was considered their usefulness.

They generally found themselves alone in wooden shacks with nothing but the pain of a lifetime of beatings and an aggravated mind to keep them company. The more fortunate ones might have been able to hitch their fate, like a wagon, to the strength and generosity of other younger Blacks who made them one of their own and found a way after a day's labor to check on them. Those left to their own devices were essentially abandoned to die in filth and agony.

The scenario is indeed less vicious in the 21st century than it was in the late 19th but the dilemma and choices concerning how we take care of the elderly or how we calmly neglect them are still just as vital. Some, in fact, would argue it is more so. People who get paid to know a great deal about population aging, along with humanitarian organizations like the United Nations and World Health Organization, have long sounded alarms on what we might look forward to as nations when it comes to anticipating the graying of populations around the world. They speak of a "crossing," now in progress, when for the first time in history the number of senior souls (65 years and older) in the world will exceed the number of children under the age of five at the same time that birth rates around the globe remain moderate or decline. Once this crossing is made, the effects of it are expected to last for at least several decades.

Americans are cautioned about the strain it will put on healthcare costs when it comes to treating the ills of a large elderly population—like that already in Canada, Japan, or Germany—and doubly warned about what this will mean for world communities where poverty is the norm rather than an exception. We are advised about the shortage of workers in certain industries following the retirement of Baby Boomers. But then are allowed to breathe an uneasy sigh of dubious relief when told influxes of immigrants could ease some of the tension when it comes to this particular problem.

Missing from official reports and recommendations are accounts of the kind of turmoil in which members of families often find themselves when they neglect to prepare for the care of an invalid matriarch or patriarch. Sons and daughters and extended family connections drift casually along until a phone call at work or in the middle of the night informs them about a parent having fallen, been assaulted by a criminal, had a heart attack, a stroke, or being found wandering in circles in a grocery store. Reality rearranges their schedule and yours. Whereas relatives may know nothing at all about the science of population aging, they understand the looming consequences of such telephone calls and many try to avoid every aspect of those consequences as much as possible. Others begin making suitable arrangements to find the just-right caregiver service, or the least scary nursing home, or they hold their breath and take the plunge to become caregivers themselves.

In my case, it was not something on which I had ever planned, especially given that the parent in question was a formidable matriarch rather than a patriarch who might have felt more comfortable with a son looking after him. And I certainly never anticipated the kinds of family divisions and conflicts it could create when it came to undeclared issues of power and authority versus responsibility, work, and personal sacrifice. Nor did I consider the financial challenges that could only become inevitable after choosing in the year 2000 to quit a job where I was earning just enough to pay professional homecare assistants to do what I had to anyway once they left. The one possibility which made it feasible for me to even consider making such an adjustment was that I might succeed well enough as an independent author to pull it off. For a time, I did.

II.

Holidays are often the most difficult for caregivers. Resentments and globs of guilt which have been boiling beneath the surface, among siblings or other family members over who has the right to do whatever whenever, can suddenly explode like overheated toxic waste. Or it can remain repressed and continue to build in poisonous intensity as loved ones grimace and chew their way through silent rage-filled gatherings. Sometimes, however, the exact opposite would occur when members would arrive and either escort our beloved matriarch to their home and bring her back later, or simply avoid the house in which I took care of her altogether. A sibling or grandchild transporting her to the location of the festivities was something I came to appreciate because it allowed time for much-needed rest and recuperation. The more acid-infused tactic of emotional isolation was one most would likely come to regret at some point.

One extended period of being noticeably shunned, from the late '90s until several years past 2000, I came to describe as the family jihad. Until 9/11, I had thought of the word jihad only in the Sufi interpretation of the battle to overcome one's most damaging spiritual weaknesses in order to achieve a higher state of divinely-inspired consciousness. After September 11, 2001, the definition proposed by violent extremists usurping the religion of Islam for their political and economic purposes caused me to shudder along with the rest of the world. Jihad should not have been applicable to a simple domestic disagreement and yet nearly every week, if not every day, the most minor issues in various households and communities escalated into conflicts that ended up as news stories about a death by stabbing, shooting, or fists.

This jihad did not involve the kind of IUDs, drones, or missile launchers used in Iraq, Yemen, and Afghanistan. It employed the type detonated by telephone calls to relatives in-state and out, to paint a skewed portrait of someone who had walked away from the activities and liberties of his own life to accommodate the needs of another's as a person terrorizing their lives and threatening the very existence of our family. How had we reached such a state? The cause of it, I thought, was mind-numbingly petty and stemmed from a grandson's—let's call him Nephew P (NCP)— insistence that a celebration be held in a home he neither owned nor rented to commemorate his job promotion.

The celebration itself—whether in the form of a cook-out, party, or sit-down dinner—was a fine enough idea. The problem was the timing and location: which was when and where I was struggling to learn how to administer my mother's fourteen medications without further impairing her well-being after she had suffered a pulmonary embolism. Suddenly, my days and nights evolved around: negotiating with my employer for extended time off, working with an agency to coordinate a routine which included receiving assistance for a few hours each morning, balancing time for research and writing with time for preparing, serving, and cleaning up after meals, and becoming accustomed to the fact that the days of my life on the south side of Savannah in a townhome that I fondly referred to as my Pyramid were now effectively over.

The most intense and unnerving attack for my side of it came when a smiling adored relative knocked on the door and, just as I opened it, rushed in with a dozen or so family jihadists behind her. Ignoring my presence altogether, they took up seats surrounding Mom in the living room, and started loudly planning what they were going to do right there in the house regardless of what had previously been said. The different medications in my mother's system made her agreeable to anything. I chose not to challenge anyone to avoid turning the situation into a story for the evening news. Sitting at the dining room table a few feet away, I tried to figure out why they felt it was appropriate to pretend I was invisible, like a stepped-on cockroach that had been swept out the door.

Upon everyone's departure an hour or so later, I did what I had been doing for quite some time: wheeled Mom into her room to use the privy, cleaned up, came back out, fixed dinner and served dinner, administered meds, watched a video, some news, and then put her to bed. The biggest change in the night for me was that after securing Mom in bed and making sure she had fallen asleep, I left the house and walked roughly two miles down to River Street. Sitting on a stone bench and leaning against a guard chain on the walkway next to the river, I stared at the water and prayed. *Heavenly Father if I made a mistake please show me how to apologize and correct it. If I was doing the right thing, show me what I need to do now.*

"They ain't gon stop 'til you spank their butts with that law."

"What!?"

Turning to see who had spoken, I saw a couple strolling by several yards away and far too busy with each other's lips to notice me.

"You made a promise and Willie Mae need you to keep it. No matter what." Again I turned. And again no one was there.

Though bright, the waxing moon was not yet full and clouds passing beneath it created strange effects on the slivers of mist above the water.

I stayed there until just before the sun began to rise, when I walked the two still-dark miles back home. Looking in on Mom, I could tell that she had remained asleep without distress and was glad about that. A homecare assistant would arrive soon, so I hurried to change clothes and make a pot of coffee.

III.

While not something I desired, the eventual fallout from the family jihad was an appearance in court. It was to be as the voice I had heard had said. I sat in one section of the courtroom by myself and the supposedly offended nephew sat in an opposite section with a dozen of his adult siblings, cousins, and friends.

The judge would not allow me to read the two-page statement I had typed up and asked that I give a brief verbal summary of why I had had certain individuals barred from the house. My intention was to do as he asked and give a quick statement about how after I had declined to host a cookout, a specific relative had convinced a group of kinspeople to show up at the house and plan the event anyway, attempting to coax my heavily-medicated mother to agree to whatever he wanted. No one was more surprised than I when I went even further and began to explain how I had taken a three-month leave of absence from my job to take care of their grandmother after she had suffered a pulmonary embolism and was now considering the possibility of quitting my job altogether to become her fulltime caregiver because the expense of paying someone else to do it and surviving the strain it was putting on me to work sixty hours a week as a store manager, and then, in addition, however many more hours as a caregiver when the paid assistant left, was creating more stress than anybody should have in their life.

"The only alternative, Your Honor, was to place her in a nursing home per her doctors' suggestion since she was going to require 24/7 monitoring for quite some time. Have you heard anybody here today say anything about being willing to compromise the quality of their lives so they can accommodate hers? Besides all of that Your Honor, some family members have insisted on dropping their young children off early in the morning for my mother, her room is close to the front door so she gets up to let them in while I'm still asleep, they drop them off for her to look after when in fact she's being taken care of by me so I end up looking after her and their children!"

The judge backed up the choice not to host a celebration at that time, said it would be best for Nephew P not to enter the house until further notice, and suggested all those present put more efforts into growing up. He also underscored the point that in light of our beloved matriarch's condition and the absence of anyone else acting as her primary caregiver, I was the recognized responsible adult authority in the house. This was oddly perplexing for a family in which our mother had first given birth to four girls, then four boys, then another girl, and another final boy, raising all of us by herself after her husband's death. With her being a widow and the four oldest offspring being female, family members were more accustomed to women directing the course of family affairs. More than once I had offered to step aside whenever anyone else was ready to take my place. For nearly a decade comprising the last years of her life, that never happened.

Nephew P did not accept the judge's directive without a final swipe at his authority: "You mean to tell me I'm not supposed to go to my grandma when she call me beggin' for help cause ain't nobody else around doin' nothin' for her?! You mean to tell me I'm just supposed to ignore her?"

Speaking with a slow clear emphasis on each word, the judge replied, "What I'm telling you… is that you need to follow the provisions outlined in the peace warrant that was issued… or else face possible charges of contempt of court and risk being arrested."

The judge's decision was not one which anybody could claim as a victory. If anything, facing off in court against people I had spent much of my adolescence helping to raise was heartbreaking. In addition, while I naively thought it clarified and settled issues, what it had really done was confirm the launch of the great family jihad. Its intensity and longevity rose to such a degree that I not only became comfortable being shunned, but welcomed the solitude that empowered my creative labors. What I did not welcome was the depression that settled over my mother when by default she became part of the collateral ostracized damage.

IV.

When the week of Thanksgiving rolled around during the fifth year of the clan jihad, I armed myself the night before with a pre-cooked smoked turkey and a box of stove-top dressing. To this, I planned to add my signature macaroni and cheese casserole, which most of my kinfolks seemed to believe was my only redeeming family value. The menu was enough to make the house smell festive with tongue-tempting savory flavors even if my mother and I would be the only ones there to enjoy it. Then the kind of magic that sparkles brightest during holidays began to shimmer and unfold.

A relative on her way out of town experienced an impulse to drop off a sweet potato pie, a cherry-glazed cheesecake, and a pot of collard greens still warm from the stove. Well that was nice, I thought, and later went to bed with a feeling of grateful contentment. A couple of hours later, I woke to the sound of Mom calling for help after she had tried to get up on her own to use the bedside commode, one footstep away, and fallen to the floor. It would take another two or three incidents of this kind to convince me to replace her treasured king-size bed with a more secure hospital-patient bed. For the time being, while everyone else was sitting up late getting drunk, smoking, preparing favorite dishes, listening to old-school tunes, and catching up on each other's news, I lifted my mother and, as gently as I could, sat her on the toilet. Another two hours would pass before being able to calm the fear and disorientation—hers as well as mine— that generally followed such events.

On Thanksgiving morning, I received a call from a fellow writer named Tiago (NCP) who had emigrated from Brazil a decade before and who was now living in Atlanta. In town to spend time with his sister Shanta (NCP) and her teenage son Cordero (NCP), he wanted to visit me as well. Knowing I would not be able to join them for dinner, he asked if I could pick them up and bring them back to my place. In Brazil, he had been a well-known radio personality and columnist, but in the United States had been working mostly in restaurant kitchens earning money to pay for his children's education back home. His sister was a homecare assistant.

We had first become friends when he attended my presentations at The Blue House Center for Creativity, where I had sometimes shared a spotlight with singer India Arie. He then later became a customer at the last bookstore I managed, and eventually someone on whom I relied when my car broke down and I needed an occasional ride home after closing the store at night. When hurricane Floyd threatened to demolish Savannah in 1999 and most residents evacuated the city (Mom among them, going to Atlanta with several of my siblings), his family and I rode out the event together, talking, laughing, and praying until the danger passed with minimal damage. With so much shared history, taking a few minutes to pick them up to join us for an afternoon Thanksgiving meal would not be a problem. Before leaving to get them, I reset the dining room table, leaving the white lace table cloth that I knew Mom preferred and replacing the sturdy stylish floral print paper plates (they would have served my purposes any day of the week) with Cotillion International China and crystal glasses. A small centerpiece and a medium-sized covered turkey gave the impression I almost knew what I was doing.

Being the generous-hearted people that they were, I anticipated Shanta getting in my 1986 Chevrolet Caprice Classic with a casserole or two. But the huge grocery store box that Tiago carried and the bulging brown bag filling Cordero's arms, I was pretty certain, was more than just a casserole. Fortunately, the back seat of the car was spacious enough to let them hold the box and bag comfortably for the short ride back from their apartment complex to the house.

Pulling up to the side of the house, I saw nephew P's car parked across the street from the front. If he was inside, it would be a violation of the judge's still-standing orders and I would have to decide what, if anything, to do about it. Unsurprisingly, when I opened the door he was on the couch next to his grandmother's chair holding a photograph that appeared to be him holding a certificate of some kind. As he stood to leave, I told my friends who he was and said that he was to be congratulated because he had worked very hard to earn another important promotion with a company where he had been working for a long time. While I kept moving towards the dining room, Shanta, as was her nature, spread her arms to embrace him and exclaimed in her musical Portuguese-speaking accent, "Oh praise be to God, that's wonderful!"

"Thank you."

It was an embrace I was not yet ready to share; yet I enjoyed the thought it might later on have some form of healing influence.

Tiago and Cordero shook Nephew P's hand as well and he called out, "Y'all have a good Thanksgiving," just before walking out the door.

Their attention then turned to Mom and she appeared as astonished as I at how effusively they praised her beauty, expressed gratitude for being welcomed into our home, and said how much they appreciated my friendship. To put her more at ease in their presence, I reminded her that these were the people who had stayed with me when a hurricane warning had forced evacuation of the city and she had gone to Atlanta with the rest of the family. She recalled hearing about them and sat up with renewed regality to receive her guests more properly. I was so floored by the sudden transformation that I didn't really notice when Shanta stepped away from us.

Suddenly I heard her say, "Oh your table is so beautiful," and then "Oh this is what we need right here." I turned to see her sit the bag they had brought onto the buffet cabinet sitting against the wall opposite the dining table. Tiago sat the box beside it. What happened next amazed me to no end as the Brazilian brother and sister began carefully unpacking one dish after another and placing it on the table: a platter of lightly-glazed ham (something my mother would enjoy sampling since I never cooked pork due to health issues), a pot of stewed codfish, a pan of rice pudding, sweet potato soufflé, Shanta's tweaked version of macaroni and cheese, chocolate cake, and peanut butter balls rolled in honey and coconut. With the food that had been gifted to us the night before, the table could not hold everything they had brought and the overflow went onto the buffet. Looking from one to the other, I turned to my friends and said, "You're a couple of Brazilian food elves."

We laughed, and I asked them to please have a seat at the table while I brought Mom over.

"Oh no Aberjhani," said Tiago, "I'll help you. We'll seed down after your mother come to the table."

"Yes we'll wait for her," said Shanta.

V.

Still mildly shaken by her fall the night before, Mom used this opportunity to bravely exercise with her walker while Tiago stood on one side of her and I on the other. The eight steps to her chair at the south-end head of the table represented an important victory of confidence over fear. I offered Tiago the seat at the north-end head of the table. He declined and said if it was okay he would like to sit next to Mom on her left side. Shanta had already taken the seat to her right and Cordero was next to his mother, so I sat at the north head-of-the-table. Shanta knew my family was quite large and asked if we should wait for whoever else was coming.

"You're the only ones I'm expecting," I said with a smile. "Anybody else can just catch up if they come. The party begins now."

The entire time Tiago did the honor of blessing the table, a smile covered my face as I looked at the abundance spread before us, so contrary to my previous plans. Putting the late composer Ja A. Jahannes' "Yes Lawd" CD on the portable player and setting the volume just below medium level, I thought, *I'm missing something here. What am I not getting?*

As we began passing dishes back and forth, Tiago and Shanta laughed and chatted like school children. Sitting so close to my mother, I thought any moment they might crawl into her lap. Huddled so closely as they were, the contrast between their skin tones stood out: my mother's a rose and pecan-brown that revealed the mixture of African and Cherokee in our bloodlines; my friends' a darker rich-coffee hue implying more African ancestry than anything else.

Knowing that Shanta, like many women immigrants from Brazil, took care of an elder six to seven days a week, I did not want her to feel obligated to serve or look after my mother. However, neither she nor Tiago would allow me to do anything about it. More than once throughout the course of our friendship, she had taken it upon herself to thank me for being bold and strong enough to endure relative poverty while taking care of my mother. There were so many, she testified, who rarely interacted with their aging parents at all except to make sure the caregiver was still on the job so they could ignore any sense of responsibility or duty of care themselves.

Shanta seemed to have been reading my mind when she looked my way and said in her rapid sing-song speech, "You get to be with her every day. In Brazil we used to be around our elders and listen to their stories all the time but here it is not like that—"

"They always had lots and lots of stories to tell us," added Tiago. "We could sit up all night listening to different kinds stories. Sometimes they were stories about how life was for them when they were younger. Sometimes they were like the stories you call…is it fairy? Fairy stories?"

"Fairy tales and folktales," said Cordero.

"Listening to their stories is probably one of the main reasons I became writer."

"And music," added Shanta. "Our grandfather played the guitar and our grandmother sang. Now Cordero plays piano. We always have fun with the elders and we haven't seen them in a long time. You see your mother every day."

"Up in the country," said the mother in question, referring to the area of Hephzibah in northwest Georgia where our people on her side of the family came from, "we would light a fire at night and listen to the radio. Hear them talk about the war, or listen to whatever the president wanted to talk about." She paused to bite a slice of ham and then, looking at Shanta, gave the highest compliment. "This ham is tender and moist, all the flavor still in it, not dried out and tough."

"Tiago cooked the meat," Shanta responded. "Everything else I cooked for you to have some traditional Brazilian food."

"Some people cook the ham too hot and too fast," said Tiago. "I steam baked it with just a little water and let it cook slow in the natural juices."

Well hell, I thought, the next time I think about sticking any kind of meat in the oven I guess I need to call Tiago first. Just as I was set to give in to a bit of envy, Cordero said, "Mmmmmm, now this what macaroni and cheese is supposed to taste like!" talking about the healthy serving he had scooped out of my dish rather than his mother's. Considering that his mother was, to my palette anyway, a world-class cook, I couldn't help smiling at the compliment.

Shanta took a nibble and added, "Oh, this is good. You've got to give me your recipe."

"It's okay, but I like yours better," I said, and placed a forkful of happiness in my mouth.

"Did you have a lot of brothers and sisters up in the country?" Tiago asked Mom.

"Four brothers and two sisters. I was the oldest girl and Buster was the oldest boy. Now it's just me and…let's see…now it's me and…and Len, the youngest. He live with his children down in Jacksonville."

"Ahhhhh," said Shanta and Tiago at the same time.

Something marvelous, just then, revealed itself and almost made me cry. My proficiency and efficiency as a caregiver was proven nearly every day. I had mastered the art of functioning as two distinct individuals: one operated on a schedule designed to meet my mother's needs and the other channeled whatever energy was left into my literary pursuits. While that worked well enough for me, it became more than obvious looking at Mom's interaction with Tiago and his family that she possibly needed more by way of social interaction than my needs and priorities could accommodate. What if the judge and I had made a mistake? What if I had fooled myself about belonging where I was and had not heard God say to me, *Do this in my name*? What if…

No: somebody had to make the hard calls and not worry about losing popularity for doing so. In this case, whether I wanted to or not, that someone had turned out to be me. And my friends had arrived on a holiday to supplement my efforts with something exhaustion had erased: a lightness of heart and spirit which had once made me believe all good things were possible as well as necessary. Perhaps it was true that being male at a spouse-less time in my life, I was not the best substitute for the generations that previously filled her holidays but like most caregivers who neglect their own lives in support of another's, I had done what I could to make them more than just tolerable. This, to me, was the very least that she had earned and deserved.

It would not have been my mother's inclination to share with our guests stories known among both immediate and extended family members about how she had taken my older siblings to Forsyth Park and other battle lines of the civil rights movement to make them face Jim Crowism head-on. She might smile and laugh but say nothing about the struggle, after being widowed at age thirty-three, to maintain employment to keep her family sheltered and fed, nor would she mention the loss of her teenage son Robert Lee to a policeman's bullet fired into his back. Hadn't Malcolm X's mother, Louise Little, lost her sanity for a time to the unrelenting stress and terror of similar situations so clearly reserved for Black men and women? She did allude to a house we had once on the city's west side where our cousins from the country would stay with us for a time until finding homes of their own or moving on to someplace in Florida or elsewhere.

The price of her ticket for survival had been the development of diabetes shortly after my birth and additional illnesses (high blood pressure, congestive heart failure, kidney failure, a thyroid condition, severe arthritis, and more) down the road. She had given so many golden bits and pieces of her life to empower the lives of others that for me the idea of ignoring her needs because they hampered my ability to tend to my own was inconceivable. It would have been easier to imagine strapping a jet-pack to my back and flying to Mars for a quick date and then returning to resume life as normal.

We were, each of us sitting at the table on Thanksgiving Day, at a crossroads of public and private dynamics which had brought us to this frame-worthy moment. I thought of the different currents and crosscurrents of history which had formed, merged, broken apart, and reformed to create the opportunity for us to give something essential to each other's lives. It was not simply that I had taken time to go get my friends and bring them back to the house. History had given birth to them in a country and time where people with their richly dark skin had been as oppressed as those of the same color in the United States.

None of us mentioned these things as we talked, ate, and laughed; they nevertheless were every bit as present as the jubilant sound of gospel music coming from my portable CD player. Added to the issue of racism was an unstable government given to periodic military coups and an inflation rate during the 1990s that reached a whopping annual percentage of 1,795–2,500 at the same time incomes were shrinking by close to 30 percent. Moreover, while developed and developing countries throughout the rest of the world still tip-toed around the reality of human trafficking in their own backyard, streets, alleyways, and roadside truck stops, Brazil's then President Fernando H. Cardoso was bold enough to acknowledge outright that some 107 years after its abolition, slavery still existed in his country and had to be eradicated.

The fear, corruption, and desperation created scenes more commensurate with something from Dante's Inferno than from the enticing colorful ads that invited the world to enjoy gorgeous beaches and exotic holidays surrounded by lush greenery on one side and luxury hotels on the other. As a result of the severe economic disparity in Brazil, Tiago had spoken to me of witnessing a family that made soup out of cardboard, water, salt, and pepper. Conditions of this kind, of course, were not restricted to his homeland. However, they were part of the reason my friends, paradoxically, eventually became guests at my Thanksgiving Day table and brought to it an abundance of joy in the form of both incredibly delicious food and their inspiring demeanor.

That they had been able to settle in Savannah was itself unusual. Their move across the Atlantic had been part of an increasing wave of immigrants from the country reaching 41,000 in the 1980s and doubling to 82,000 in the 1990s. Most of these had settled in the Northeast in places like Massachusetts or New York, or out west in California. Another large group was in Florida, but history is a lover of grand epics as well as small miracles and therefore allows for exceptions. Moreover, it dawned on me that at the very moment when I was considering how blessed I was to have them there making Mom laugh and allowing me to fill my stomach with stewed codfish and coconut-honey-coated peanut butter balls, at that very moment, others from their country were being apprehended at the US-Mexico border for trying to enter the country illegally.

Things could easily have gone a different way for them just as they could have for Mom, our extended family, and me. My intention had never been to remain in Savannah for the decades I inevitably would after separating from the U.S. Air Force. Each day seemed to bring a confrontation with one ghost of the past after another. Ghosts, in fact, seemed to be a homegrown specialty of the city. None loomed more menacingly across the landscape than that of Eugene Talmadge, the four-time governor of Georgia who had enjoyed tremendous popularity driven by his unrepentant passion for promoting white supremacy and for whom the bridge spanning across the Savannah River onto Hutchinson Island was declared a memorial. As much as Savannahians and Georgians apparently liked to believe the kind of racial discrimination that made the passage of civil rights laws necessary in the 1960s no longer existed, Talmadge's name attached so lovingly to the beautiful 1.9-mile bridge made it a virtual monument to racism.

VI.

We were, all of us sitting there at the Thanksgiving table, refugees of a kind. We had escaped from the dangers of pain poured over our lives like molten steel, the threat of imminent abandonment, and fear of an eclipsed future. Out of all of us, I could not help focusing on my mother and wondering about the millions like her who were no less deserving to be surrounded by love as she was right now, but who were not. Within my research on subjects which fell under the domain of sociological imagination, I had started to come across the term "duty of care," or sometimes "duty to care." It meant what it sounded like it did: in situations where the least capable among us were in peril due to extreme adverse social conditions, then societies and individuals not in such peril were ethically obligated to help ease their anguish and reduce their vulnerability. The problem from at least one perspective was that the duty to care did not necessarily equate to a capacity to care—or an ability to exercise empathy.

The world was flooded with people whose sole focus would only ever be on themselves. This condition was not new: it was what made slavery, rape, institutional corruption, murder, and the gravest betrayals all possible. Regardless of scalding contempt hurled in their direction, they might be persuaded to behave in a specific manner but would only feel a certain way if inspired from within. What would life look like in a world where one large segment of earth's inhabitants desperately needed the assistance of another segment for whom the practice and concept of caring was completely alien? Was it possible we were staring blindly at such a world already and refusing to realize it? How close were we to condemning millions to the experience of slaves who had been left to slowly rot in a wooden shed of misery and indignity? The silent screams of too many would suggest that they had already crossed over into a zone of highly-refined damnation and, so far as they could tell, were in danger of remaining there even after taking their very last breath. The laughter, chatter, and aromas which spilled from my table one special Thanksgiving Day had proven we had much better options than simply existing in hell.

Forsyth Park Confederate Monument in Savannah the morning after Hurricane Matthew struck the city in 2016. (photo by Aberjhani)

Trees down Everywhere

"Each root and branch of the tree represented a different force or power. The roots represented earthly forces and powers, the Earthly Mother, the Angel of Earth, the Angel of Life, the Angel of Joy, the Angel of the Sun, the Angel of Water and the Angel of Air."

—Edmond Bordeaux Szekely

To leave Savannah and avoid hurricane Matthew's *Biblical* fury or not to leave Savannah and risk the storm's predicted unsparing rage? That was the nerve-racking question in need of a quick answer on Friday, October 7, 2016. Previously, almost sixty-nine years to the day, on October 15, 1947, area residents faced a similar dilemma when confronted by the Cape Sable hurricane. Early predictions were that the erratically-swerving Cape Sable threat would bypass the city; a revised practically last-minute forecast gave residents of nearby Tybee Island and surrounding vicinities less than twelve hours to escape before it hit. Robocalls going out to Savannah residents on Thursday, October 6, 2016, had suggested they get moving as soon as possible to avoid an early Saturday-morning collision with Matthew.

Exactly how lucky was I feeling?

For the Cape Sable hurricane, government officials—the U.S. Army Corps, Air Force, National Weather Bureau, and Office of Naval Research—concocted a plan known as Project Cirrus to outsmart the storm by attempting to modify its trajectory, and force the squall to move away from Savannah, two days before landfall. The idea was to "seed" the maelstrom by making several drops of large chunks of dry ice into its rain bands and thereby alter the density of cloud moisture, theoretically decreasing the power of its expected punch. Nothing of the kind had ever been attempted before and some people later claimed the experiment caused the hurricane to move toward Savannah instead of sending it in the opposite direction. True or not, the *Savannah Evening Press* would later inform its readers, "Hurricane winds which reached a velocity of at least 95 miles an hour lashed Savannah and Vicinity early this morning, felling trees, unroofing houses, smashing windows and advertising signs and scattering debris over the streets. There were no casualties reported."

The financial cost of damage to some 1,500 buildings was more than $3 million. The psychological cost to the local population was perhaps immeasurable due to the last-minute sounds of sirens and loud-speakers warning people that a hurricane scheduled to travel west had changed its mind and was now making a beeline for their front doors. That the cost in human lives was negligible might qualify as divine intervention for those inclined to think that way. Just unbelievably lucky for those who think otherwise.

II.

The decision to leave or stand my ground against nature had been easier to make in September 1999 when hurricane Floyd came roaring up the Atlantic coast and sent roughly 90 percent of the city's population scrambling on all roads leading elsewhere. That was a period when I tended to rely heavily on my instincts and made certain emergency decisions based on two things: the first was accumulated images recorded in my dream notebook the week before a given date; the second was any objective scientific or physical evidence to back up whatever I determined my intuition was telling me. Despite the pronounced dramatized anxiety concerning category 3 hurricane Floyd so evident in the voices of area meteorologists, my entire being insisted on remaining calm and stationary.

Suppose, however, that soothing sense of tranquility was just a side effect of my daily meditation and I was coaxing myself into a state of deadly denial? For such a potentially catastrophic event, I needed something more than intuitive persuasion. The moment of conviction came when at least two meteorologists reported a high air pressure mass (or was it a low one?) was moving out of Canada toward the lower southern and southeastern regions of the United States. When I saw the line drawn like an arc curved toward the southeast on the weather map, I was immediately convinced it would somehow shield the area from Floyd and said loud enough for all within earshot, including my mother and eldest brother, to hear, "There's our angel right there."

The call for voluntary evacuation of the city came on Monday, September 13, and for mandatory evacuation the next day. While comfortable with my decision so far as it impacted only me, I did not try to convince anyone else to follow my lead. Predictions remained steady that Savannah was expected to take either a direct hit from the hurricane or a crippling blow from its expansive outer bands. I focused my thoughts by writing the following in a journal at noon on Tuesday, September 14, 1999:

…With the threat of hurricane Floyd as predicted charging up the east coast half the [people in the] city (or more) have left… I put Mom on the road with my sister, brother-in-law, and their family at noon yesterday. The original plan was for them to go to our cousins in Waynesboro, or rather to hotels in that area, but every hotel and motel was booked solid so they wound up making the trip all the way to Atlanta. Normally that would have been a four-hour deal with the attendant ordinary levels of stress. Yesterday, however, was not an ordinary day, and with the city undergoing a mass exodus traveling was not easy. Even before getting out of the city, travelers had to contend with the fact that every street leading to a westward interstate was clogged bumper to bumper for miles. 37th and Gwinnett Streets had lines of cars stretching from the west side exit points all the way down to East Broad Street. As I drove eastward on 37th, I couldn't believe the number of cars lined up block after block reaching from one side of the city to the next…

Aside from wanting to test the accuracy of my instincts about Floyd as well as hoping to steal, from a distance, a glance at his ferocity, I had also chosen to stay in the event friends who had made the same decision might need to pool resources for survival. Miriam K. Center and the late Bill Bagwell, both writers, felt the hurricane might draw near but believed it was not interested enough in Savannah to make landfall in the historic original colony. There was also concern for my new immigrant friends from Brazil: Tiago, his sister Shanta, and her son Cordero. Already strangers in a strange southern land, they were reluctant to get on evacuation buses without knowing precisely where they might end up or when they would be coming back.

To partially put my mother's mind at ease, I accepted my sister's and brother-in-law's suggestion that I stay at their house while they hit the road because it was newer with better wiring, a reinforced roof, and built on higher ground. My own dwelling on the opposite side of town was closer to Tybee Island and therefore more susceptible to flooding if the expected direct hit came. Tiago, Shanta, and Cordero in turn accepted an invitation to join me. As a result, we spent a fun two days watching videos, listening to music, and getting to know each better.

My friends were surprised when I showed them a movie in Spanish, directed by Nicolas Echevarria, called *Cabeza De Vaca*. They at first had a good laugh when I pronounced the title, which Shanta translated for me as "The Cow's Head," because until looking at the video cover for themselves they assumed I had misread it. After watching the film with its heavily metaphysical imagery symbolizing the physical journey and personal evolution of sixteenth-century Spanish explorer Alvar Nunez Cabeza de Vaca, we better understood the significance of the title.

We kept the video party rolling by watching Kate Winslet and Leonardo DiCaprio fall in love and battle against disaster in the extended 194-minute double-cassette edition of *Titanic*. And then we smiled throughout Massimo Troisi's performance as postman Mario Ruoppolo, and Philippe Noiret's as poet Pablo Neruda, in *Il Postino-The Postman*, directed by Michael Radford.

All in all, it was a good teachable cross-cultural moment.

Once Tiago and I got up courage enough to venture out into the gray soggy uneasy calm, we discovered the electricity had gone out in both our homes. Naturally, we raided the refrigerators for perishables and took them back with us to where, for whatever inexplicable reason, the power never went out. The direct hurricane hit, we were grateful to note, did not come this time. Instead of plunging our lives into wind-tossed chaos, Floyd delivered a break from our daily struggles. It also came to represent one of those extraordinary occasions of inexplicable good fortune, such as when General Tecumseh Sherman chose not to burn Savannah to the ground near the end of the Civil War, which allowed the colony to survive and perpetuate its description as a seemingly immortal city. Indeed, any number of hurricanes would continue causing Savannahians to alternately gasp with anticipation of destruction and later exhale with prayerful relief. After being spared by Floyd, Shanta may have expressed our little group's thrilled amazement best when she said, "I can't believe we're having such a good time because of that hurricane. Praise Jesus Christ."

III.

With hurricane Matthew, seventeen years later as the first week of October 2016 drew to a close, mandatory calls were made to evacuate the barrier islands several days before the "strongly-recommended" but non-mandatory evacuation of Savannah. People were advised to leave the city and Chatham Area Transit buses provided transportation for residents to either take them to shelters at locations in town or hop on a second fleet of older tour buses heading northwest to Augusta.

Matthew had proven impressive enough to gain the respect of populations in several different countries. Heartbreaking images coming out of Haiti were unforgettable: a man walking through water up to his calves while carrying a woman on his back; lines of people holding on to each pulling through washed-out streets; a woman and child sitting on the crumbled remains of their home and waiting for someone to come tell them what they should do. So why wasn't my feeling about leaving or staying not as clear this time around as it had been with hurricane Floyd?

Prior to forecasts about Matthew's looming threat, I had been making some real progress on a book project that meant a lot to me and maybe my focus on it was blocking out everything else. Then the decision was made for me when Vanda, a brilliant but physically-challenged friend nineteen years my senior, called and told me she was still at home alone. I forced myself not to scream with panic through the phone when asking why she thought that was a good idea. Being a strong-willed woman who was once a leading foot-soldier in Savannah's 1960s Civil Rights Movement, she found it difficult to think of herself as vulnerable in any given situation. Like so many others who marched beside her—and like the battlefield veterans of Vietnam, Iraq, and Afghanistan—she had been forever molded by her identity as a sentry on duty to ignore any danger to herself and concentrate on protecting others. As admirable as such a disposition might be, it was not going to work in this case.

We had a passionate debate about how she could stay in Savannah with her son Moses and his family but could not remain alone in her east-side two-story Victorian District home built in 1900.

"But what about you?!" she countered. "I don't want you getting hurt if it gets real bad."

"Don't worry about me, I can still hustle and scramble if I need to. You can't."

"I don't like to get in people way just because of a hurricane."

"What do you mean get in people's way? You're going to give your son a heart attack if he has to worry about you in this house by yourself with a category 3 hurricane about to hit the city. This isn't like when Floyd came and stayed forty miles offshore then shot up north to—

where'd it go? —to North Carolina, didn't it? Matthew's only going to be eighteen to twenty-five miles offshore. It's been zig-zagging back and forth, east and west, and one good zig or zag to the west could wipe Savannah out. Didn't you see what it did to Haiti?"

"Well what chu gon do?"

"I tell you what, you go with your son Moses and I'll stay at your place since your two-story house might be a little safer than my one-story. I'll watch it until you get back. How about that?"

"Well why can't I stay here with—"

"Because I'm going to call your son right now and tell him what we just decided. We're not going to argue about this anymore, okay? Please?!"

"Alright then. Alright. I love you."

"I love you too my friend, and I'll see you in a little while."

"I'll see you too if the Lord say so."

"Let's hope He does."

The original plan was to make our multiple moves later that afternoon, Thursday, October 6. We decided, however, to give ourselves until Friday morning to get better organized and more thoroughly secure valuables we would hate to lose but could not take with us. The projected timeline for the hurricane's arrival in or near Savannah was 1 a.m. Saturday morning and we guessed the outer bands of heavier rain and winds would not reach the area until past noon on Friday. What I disliked more than anything else was the idea of losing an entire day of writing to Matthew, especially since all indications were that this time around we more than likely would get a good strong side-swipe even if we managed to once again dodge the bullet of a direct hit. That, in turn, was going to mean a power outage lasting anywhere from a couple of days to a week or more. Shit.

Refusing to go down without a last-minute ditch effort, I made a fresh pot of coffee, plugged my Handycam into the computer to recharge, and started typing. If the hurricane were to suddenly pick up speed, move faster and hit harder than anyone anticipated, take me by surprise and end my literary endeavors along with all others at the keyboard— well then, whoever felt like it could later say I left the world doing what I believed I had been born to do: writing.

The cypher kept rolling and the syllables kept flowing up until midnight. The time had come to start dismantling my desktop computer with the speakers, printer, phone, and batteries, put everything in cushioned boxes, and then place those in the most hurricane-proof closets in the house. This turned out to be one of the better moves I could have made and something now considered a gift of the hurricane. One of the closets which I had decided would make a good storage unit had been blocked for years by two book cases. I could not remember what exactly was inside and feared that upon opening it I might discover some unwelcome creatures had built their home there. Squirrels could have invaded it. Rats maybe. Two summers ago a possum had run through the back yard and disappeared beneath the house. Possibly a family of snakes or an orphan alligator could be in there. Damn. All this anxiety was hurricane Matthew's fault.

Sliding the book shelves to the side, I pulled the closet door open and quickly jumped back. Sitting on its floor were two old briefcases and a box filled with magazines and something that looked like several silk-embroidered research journals or notebooks. I picked up two of the journals and quickly looked at the dates inside. One was dated November 17, 1993 - April 7, 1994, and the other April 8, 1994 – August 25, 1994. Had I really gotten so lucky? Finding the dreaded alligator or possum behind that door would have been less astounding than rediscovering these notebooks. Each one contained handwritten accounts of initial book-signing events with author John Berendt, the late celebrity drag queen Lady Chablis, and the late singer Nancy Hillis (a.k.a. Mandy) all of *Midnight in the Garden of Good and Evil* fame. Chablis and Hillis had both only recently passed. I had been using, as part of my research for the book in progress, one set of journals from the 1990s to complete an essay about my interactions with the people who had made Berendt's *Midnight* so infamously famous but to fill in certain gaps needed one very important volume: November 17, 1993-April 7, 1994. Now it was found and could be used to verify and supplement passages written strictly from memory.

If I were anything resembling a fashionista I would have packed to take with me my largest suitcase stuffed with my most treasured and (under the circumstances) maybe functional clothing items . Being who and what I am, my most spacious piece of luggage was instead crammed with irreplaceable rare-edition books, more notebooks on literary happenings in Savannah during the 1990s, military records, irreplaceable photographs that had never been scanned to digital file, copies of the *Poetry Society of Georgia Yearbook*, and a first-run galley for my first book: *I Made My Boy Out of Poetry*. By the time I finished stuffing the suitcase, it was heavy enough to roll in front of one of the designated survivor closets and trust that it would withstand whatever force might rage against it.

That left to take with me a 20x14 smaller version of the large suitcase and my leather shoulder bag with its very useful built-in one dozen pockets and lined folders. A change of clothing with extra socks and underwear were automatic choices for the overnighter. What else should I cram into it and my shoulder bag in case the hurricane hit Savannah even half as hard as it did Haiti, and, if I was to stand a chance at putting my life halfway back together afterwards? All of my assorted computer thumb drives, one larger portable drive, and a cassette tape-MP3 player/converter all went into a plastic zip-lock bag. A battery-powered lamp with extra batteries fit neatly between the clothes and notebooks. On top of these went legal papers and another shirt.

My shoulder bag expanded in its normal capacity as a mobile office with folders and pockets containing manuscripts, ink pens, pencils, a camcorder, retractable photo-video tripod, cough drops, vitamins, folded umbrella, more legal papers, a copy of "occasional prose" essays by Flannery O'Connor (important to my research) and yes, more notebooks. Taking another quick scan around me, a volume of *Delicious Laughter, Rambunctious Teaching Stories from the Mathnawi* by Jelaluddin (or Jalal al-Din) Rumi, as interpreted by poet Coleman Barks, caught my attention. How had I overlooked it?

Making room in my bag to slide *Delicious Laughter* inside, it was obvious that humor would be as essential to my survival as unyielding shelter, fresh water, or anything else over the next few days. On the second page of the book, Barks had written my name with what appeared to be shimmering gold acrylic paint, circled the title of the book and signed it "With Love" using the same brilliant color. Beneath the word love, his name, Coleman, was written in plain black ink and dated "1/20/91." He had sent the book after I wrote him proposing a theory that James Baldwin's writings may have been influenced by Rumi's to some degree during his visits to Turkey. After receiving my letter, he had called me and we talked about the possibility, of which I had no proof. More than anything else, we discussed this second or third re-introduction of Rumi—within the past century—to the American public occurring at the time, and the impact it was having on my life as a bookseller and as a poet. Bark's name signed in *Delicious Laughter* was one of the touchstones of my life, and had reinforced the will and inspiration to share my voice as a poet on the page and on the stage.

IV.

Early the next morning, Friday, I was awakened by rain splashing through leaves and onto the metal roof. It became immediately apparent we had miscalculated how quickly the outer bands of Matthew's 500-mile-wide intense embrace would reach Savannah. Coordinating with Moses over the phone, he soon picked me up in his SUV and we headed to his mother's house. Standing at five-feet-nine and weighing in at around 250 pounds, Vanda did not allow us to carry her down the front steps. We stood guard with Moses's daughter Tara as she held onto the rail and made her way down the steps under her own insistent power. After settling into the car with Tara, essential medications, luggage, and other equipment went into the SUV. One last kiss and she was on her way to the other side of town, a part much closer to an interstate access route if one should be needed, with her son and granddaughter.

It was early enough in the day, around noon or so, that the wind and rain remained sporadic, alternating between light showers and quick moderately heavy bursts, not posing (for the time being) a threat to surrounding structures or the lives still inside many of them. I had been to Vanda's house many times before and was accustomed to usually congregating in a single large downstairs room near the back of the house, close to the kitchen, where everything she required was placed no further than a few steps away. This time, having to consider the possibility of needing to "hunker down," as the meteorologists were saying, in a safe space, I took greater notice of the layout. A staircase to the left led to the four bedrooms (now rarely used) on the second floor and a long hallway beside it opened onto three entrances leading to three large rooms; each of these in turn were separated by wide open arches leading from one room to the other. At the end of the hallway was a small dining area followed by the kitchen, and just off to the right of the kitchen a closet-sized foyer before reaching the back door and porch. A litter box for Vanda's cat, "Miss Kitty," sat beneath a wall cabinet in the foyer.

My friend had spoken often about how as a young woman she bought the house back in the early 1960s after marrying a widower with seven sons and one daughter. It had cost her four figures and was now valued at six. Much of its furnishings had been discarded antiques Vanda had retrieved and restored herself. She had resisted efforts at predatory gentrification and watched with interest as the block where she became a mainstay matriarchal figure to generations evolved from one occupied solely by African Americans to one designated part of the city's Victorian District and where she was the last black person on it.

From an architectural perspective, the large gorgeous finely-crafted windows in each of the beautiful high-ceilinged first-floor rooms were breathtaking. From the viewpoint of a would-be hurricane survivor, they could prove every bit as deadly as the gang members' and policemen's bullets that had been steadily taking the lives of African American men, women, and children all over the country. Where exactly could I hunker down in a building which had been designed almost 120 years ago as a model of refined elegance rather than as a demonstration of strength or fortitude against one of nature's most destructive forces? My best bet, should such a point arrive, likely would be to take shelter in the bathroom beneath the staircase.

For the next few hours, all remained relatively quiet and I spent my time alternating between reading the notebooks I had brought with me, making new entries in a current journal, and mostly watching local meteorologist Jeff Kirk's updates on Matthew's imminent strike. Reports had come in estimating a quarter of a million Georgians were already without power. Taking advantage of the fact that mine, or rather Vanda's, was still on, I began studying the different plaques, awards, and certificates of appreciation mounted on the hallway wall. They had been presented in honor of Vanda's participation in Savannah's Civil Rights Movement throughout the latter half of the previous century and for her ongoing leadership within several sorority and fraternity organizations in the twenty-first. These honors possibly told more of the story of her black-woman's life than many of the numerous other events and twists of fate that had shaped her character and given substance to her biography.

Through her "work with the organizations," such as the Southern Christian Leadership Conference, Order of the Eastern Star, Heroines of Jericho, and Feed the Hungy, she had labored beside members around the world to help correct different forms of social injustice—like poverty, racism, and sexism—that persisted no matter how many people gave years of their lives battling to defeat them. A lot of her efforts in more recent years had consisted of privately funding a scholarship to help young women complete college. Although people such as the iconic Rep. John Lewis had acknowledged her invaluable contributions to "the movement," she was among the mostly unsung black heroines who had done everything from emptying their purses to fund crucial campaigns, to spending time in jail for however long only to get out and head straight back to the front lines.

Looking at the gleaming acknowledgements lining the wall, the thought of them getting buried beneath a pile of Victorian rubble nagged at my conscience and I started wondering where I might find a box in which to store them until the danger passed. If it passed. Thinking I might have seen something I could use in a corner of the back-door foyer, I walked to the kitchen. Hearing something odd, I stopped at the entrance to the foyer. The noise came again:

Plip-plop.

The sound of a drop of water hitting the floor disturbed me so much that I tried to pretend I had not heard it. I took another step. Then more came: p*lip-plop, plip-plop, plip-plop, plip-plop.* On a small ledge running across the wall above the back door, several shiny drops grew fatter and prepared to drop: Plop! Plop! Plop! A small pool of water had already formed in a large industrial-type mop bucket standing against the wall and another pool had started building up on the floor in front of the door. Suddenly the sound of the wind and rain beating against the house magnified by what felt like fifty decibels. Something told me it actually had been coming down hard for a while but I had noticed neither it nor how much time had passed since my arrival at the house. Even though it was nearly midnight—or was it past already? —the power was still on

So far, the mop bucket had caught most of one leak; I needed something else for a second and rushed to find a plastic washbasin to place behind the bucket. It felt, for a moment, like a major disaster had been averted. Then I turned to walk back through the kitchen and my gaze traveled up to the shape of a large bowl beginning to extend from the white ceiling. From the very center of this weirdly expanding bowl, a bright pearl of water fell and was soon followed by another. Then another, and another, and another. Quickly, I grabbed a green plastic bucket beside the washing machine and placed it beneath the bulge in the ceiling. Why the odd swelling made me think of paintings by Salvador Dali and graffiti art by Banksy is a mystery.

That's not good, I thought, staring up at the danger.

Going back into the main side room, I turned on the television for updates on the hurricane's proximity to Savannah. Instead, I got CNN news anchor Wolf Blitzer showing a video of then Republican presidential candidate Donald Trump talking to television entertainment reporter Billy Bush about grabbing women by their genitals.

Wait, that can't be what he said.

When I flipped the channel to Fox News and found another anchor commenting on the same issue, and comparing it to a new batch of Hillary Clinton emails that had been hacked and released by WikiLeaks, the house suddenly felt like it was rushing down a cliff in a horrendous mudslide. What I was hearing combined with the increased intensity of the storm made me think for a second that I might have suffered some kind of psychological break with reality. Clicking again through channels, I found a local station to confirm what I had finally realized. It was already past midnight and the hurricane was approaching its maximum impact zenith. That fact alone was more than enough drama for one night but I could not resist flipping back to CNN and Fox to learn more about what my brain kept insisting I could not have heard. And why did I do that? There again was Blitzer, but this time talking with a panel of women, one of whom could barely hold back her anger, about the leaked video.

Miss Kitty the cat, whom I had not seen all evening, suddenly walked through the door, looked sharply in my direction, then went out again. Maybe she could not believe it either.

What had been said by Donald Trump and then made public by *The Washington Post* was indefensible. It would (I incorrectly assumed) undoubtedly damage Mr. Trump's political aspirations as well as other spheres of engagement. In fact, any number of Americans were apparently shrugging their shoulders and saying it was no big deal. Understanding the casual joviality with which he had made the unsettling statements in 2005, the year he turned 59 years old and Billy Bush 34, was extremely difficult. So was resisting the urge to take a chance turning on Vanda's computer and responding to this nightmare on social media. Between the revelation of the genital-grabbing comment and the increasing strength of the storm battering the house, the concept of hell on earth began to take on some strange new surrealistic meanings. As Michelle Obama would say later, it had "shaken me to my core."

Of all the images the situation brought to mind, the most persistent was not of the Republican presidential candidate doing what he said he could do because "stars" got away with it. The most powerful image, oddly enough, was of his chosen would-be vice president, Mike Pence. In addition to the statements he had made in defense of his political partner, Pence's quiet declaration of Christian faith and moral principles had made him one of the more serenely gallant, loyal, and admirable figures in the race for the White House regardless of party affiliation. Yet how could the pearls of grace and wisdom he had brought to the table retain any value when they were constantly being sloshed with more and more foul-smelling slime? If anyone deserved better—aside from the American people themselves and women as a whole—it seemed to me at that moment that it might have been this man who had proven to be such a capable champion and ally.

The way the video had been made public was as troubling as its contents. Criticizing the intended negative impacts of guerrilla decontextualization had comprised a large percentage of my writings about attacks against President Barack Obama during his second presidential campaign and throughout his presidency in general. Did this kind of "leak" fall into the same category or was it something different because of what it implied (should one say revealed?) about the character of a man seeking to occupy one of the most powerful political offices in the world? He had, somewhat semi-apologetically, referred to his recorded crudity as "locker room banter," and the obvious problem was it had not taken place in a locker room. It had occurred in the company of a known media personality while en route to making an appearance on a popular TV soap opera. Therefore, the context was not as far removed as in more blatant examples of guerrilla decontextualization—like the infamous attempt to portray the Rev. Jeremiah Wright as a dangerously violent left-wing radical and thereby labeling President Obama the same via their past association.

Invasions and exploitations of individuals' private lives had become a too-common feature of what passed for journalism in the digital age. Was such a strategy, generally practiced in collusion with hackers of the more criminal-minded or self-aggrandizing variety, any less a type of industry corruption than the acts which their targets were accused of committing? Did they help to enforce ethical standards? Or did they simply manipulate them to certain individuals' personal benefits and unchecked arrogance?

The sound of something falling against the house—a tree limb or dead body maybe—pulled my attention back to the environmental situation at hand and once again I walked to the back of the house to see how the rain-catching buckets were doing. Not good. The three containers were nearly full and more leaks had developed, including an aggressive trickle sliding down through the socket of the uncovered light bulb in the vestibule ceiling and another at the top of the entryway.

No less alarming was the growing swelling hanging from the kitchen ceiling itself as if it was about to give birth to a small planet. Earlier, drops of water had been seeping through every few seconds. Now it was turning into a steady stream much like a broken faucet.

The first order of business was to pray that the water dripping through the light bulb socket did not mean I was going to get electrocuted if I stepped onto the wet floor beneath it. The second was to open the back door, drag the larger industrial mop bucket onto the porch with its not-so-steady floor boards, and empty it onto the steps without the wind blowing it back on me. Looking at the branches of magnolias, palm trees, and oaks swaying and shaking in different neighbors' yards, I recalled the famous passage that gave Zora Neale Hurston's classic Harlem Renaissance novel its title: *Their Eyes Were Watching God.* The hurricane that Hurston's heroine, Janie, witnessed was probably more devastating than Matthew but it was also one that a reader could make go away just by closing the book. We could not do that with Matthew.

My third move was to empty the basin next to the mop bucket and then the plastic pail in the kitchen. The steady stream coming through the kitchen ceiling forced me to switch the bucket out for a taller deeper twenty-quart plastic trash can. No, it had not been designed to catch water pouring through a ceiling but it certainly rose to the repurposed occasion. I slid the mop around to get up however much water I could, and then remembered seeing a package of a dozen or more rolls of paper towels in the second side room. A few thick-folded wads made excellent pads to wipe the floors and place around the buckets to absorb whatever the containers missed. With the increased leakage, another large basin and a rectangular plastic clothes hamper were recruited to stop an overflow from spilling into the kitchen and streaming down the hallway to the front door. This adventure, if I could make myself consider it one, was completely different from the time shared with my Brazilian friends when Floyd remained far enough off shore for us to enjoy a private film festival, feast on Shanta's excellent cooking, and laugh ourselves silly.

At least once every hour for the next several, I ignored the angry ache in my spine and repeated the established procedure of emptying containers out the back door and replacing the paper towel pads as needed. Stepping into the foyer without getting wet was impossible and I never became 100 percent certain that the water dripping through the light bulb socket might not trigger some kind of electrical death charge. The biggest concern was maintaining a state of readiness in the event the distended bulge in the ceiling burst. More than likely, the trash can beneath it would catch most of the water; however, what else might drop with it was an unknown. I had never been up to the second floor of the house and had no idea what was above the kitchen or whether it was making matters worse. Moreover, there was no guarantee the entire second floor itself might not come crashing down onto, or get blown away with, the first.

Meteorologists had said the hurricane would approach its zenith around 1 a.m. It did precisely that. This was also when exhaustion swallowed all of my muscles along with my mind and I fell asleep in a leather office chair in front of the computer.

Whether it was Miss Kitty the cat brushing against my leg that woke me up three hours later or something else I'm not sure. Whatever it was did so barely in time for me to hurry and empty the containers again before they could spill over. The plastic trash can was the only one not in danger of overflowing. Having averted the flood yet again, I went this time to the front of the house and opened the first elegantly-sculpted wooden door. Then, reaching to unlock the outer plexiglass door, I stopped as I noticed something shiny resting flat against it on the other side. A dragonfly sat motionless with its long tail stretched out straight behind it and silvery wings spread out on either side like sparkling jewels.

What amazed me the most? Was it seeing a dragonfly, period, in the 4 AM darkness? Or was it realizing that the insect was not moving the slightest while hurricane Matthew still howled all around us, ripping limbs off of trees and crashing them onto cars and houses? If nothing else, its gossamer-like wings should have shredded right off its tiny slender body. Yet as I stood there wide awake and staring, they did not. Then an odd thought came out of nowhere: *It looks like a dragonfly. Anybody can see that. Only maybe it's not a dragonfly.* That was silly. What else could something that looks like a dragonfly pressed against a plexiglass door at 4 AM in the middle of a hurricane be if not an actual dragonfly?

Slowly closing and locking both doors, I turned to walk back down the hallway. Two or three steps and, for the first time, the lights went out. Total darkness. The hallway provided a straight shot to the kitchen and adjacent room where I had set up shop and left my portable lamp. Once back in the leather reclining office chair-bed, it struck me how lucky it had been that the power stayed on for as long as it did. Had it gone out earlier in the evening, making the trips back and forth to empty buckets would have been a lot harder. Maybe impossible. As it was, if the predicted timeline for the hurricane held true, it should start pulling away from Savannah over the next hour and further diminish the chance of in-house flooding or of the ceiling collapsing. The best thing to do would be to go to sleep and wait for what the morning might bring.

V.

Almost five hours later, the first thing I noticed as my eyes slowly creaked open was the dull brightness of light shining behind the dark green window shade. It may not have been the full-on brilliance of early morning pale gold but it was a startling contrast to the darkness that had ruled all creation only hours before. The electricity was still out and that made me glad I had brought along a battery-operated CD player with a radio. None of the stations I normally listened to in the city were broadcasting and I scrolled up and down the FM dial until hearing an announcer say "Alpha Storm Central is now live on all six of our Alpha Media Radio Stations."

Well thank you Alpha Storm Central.

He was taking calls from people throughout the coastal area Low Country sharing reports on how hard their neighborhoods had been hit or how miraculously one side of a street had been spared while another had been totally trashed. Whether calling in from the Southside, Midtown, the Historic District, East Savannah, West Savannah, Thunderbolt, Wilmington Island, Sandfly, Pinpoint, or Hilton Head (South Carolina), the statements most common to every story were "the power's still out," and, "trees are down everywhere. Never seen nothing like it in Savannah. Every street you turn on, trees torn up out the dirt with their roots showing. Never seen nothing like it."

They claimed to have heard reports of sustained winds gusting anywhere from sixty to more than 100 miles per hour. The focus was solely on the amazement of the moment and no one offered comparisons to previous hurricanes. Nevertheless, the repeated emphasis on destroyed trees reminded me of the reports of devastation that followed Cape Sable's 95-miles per hour onslaught. Unlike the ancient entities known as the Ents in J.R.R. Tolkien's *Lord of the Rings* trilogy, the living plants in our non-fantasy environmentally-challenged world could neither speak up for themselves nor hurl boulders at those whose pollution-producing habits were endangering their lives.

Sitting around and waiting to see or hear what happened next was not something I could do so I grabbed my shoulder bag and camcorder and headed for beautiful Forsyth Park, only a few blocks away. Opening the interior wooden door to go out, I noticed the dragonfly I had seen pressed against the outer plexiglass door was no longer there. Then, stepping outside, I looked up and down the street and saw that Vanda's east Park Avenue block had been among the luckier areas. The scenario changed walking a block to the west where half a magnolia tree stretched across the pavement and someone yelled to warn me about the long power line snaking out beneath it toward the curb. Over to the north on Waldburg Street there was another tree, an elm it looked like, on top of a car.

Going west again toward Abercorn, a palm tree that had stood about thirty-five feet tall the day before was now fallen across the road, its trunk cracked at the base and its shaggy green head resting in peace against concrete. The sight unnerved me in a way I had not anticipated. A slow burning gathered in my chest as I lifted the Handycam to take a photo while simultaneously blinking away tears. Why was I crying looking at this tree?

A young blond woman on a bike stopped to take pictures also and I wondered what the image meant, besides an interesting quick post to Facebook or Snapchat, to her. The sturdy low-quarter boots on her feet and canvas utility backpack against her spine made me think she might be more eco-conscious than some and therefore saw the once-stately fallen palm as the victim of a renegade force caused by man-made climate change. It could be that she saw it not as emblematic of a possible future, but as confirmation of an embattled present.

Matthew's erratic path and extended life as it continued up the coast toward North Carolina had provided ample reason to believe it was a spawn of global warming. Its ability to sustain winds between categories 3 and 5 statuses for more than a week was particularly fascinating. And troubling. New Age soothsayers during the 1990s had spoken of a time in the twenty-first century when instead of extreme atmospheric disturbances dying out a few days after forming, we would begin to see the development of super hurricanes and super tornadoes that would last longer and cause much more destruction over larger geographical areas like vengeful wraiths refusing to die. Some, they claimed, could become permanent fixtures on the planet and transport their deadly rage from continent to continent for years. Here again, Matthew had provided some sense of such a possibility, passing over both Haiti and Cuba without losing any of its formidable strength, or diminishing for a short while and then exploding all over again into a major terror. Could it be because of something we had all done by pretending not to know better?

For me, the uprooted palm tree had once been of such living majesty that it was another kind of earthling. Looking at it stretched out across the street, I saw a dead body which had been made lifeless by deadly disregard running amok in the world.

"You think that's something," said a man passing by, "you need to go up to Forsyth Park. About fifteen trees been knocked down."

"Really? Fifteen?"

"Yeah man. Might be more than that."

Visualizing the image of more than a dozen trees "knocked down" in Forsyth Park was painful. For one of the earliest versions of my novel *Songs from the Black Skylark zPed Music Player*, Forsyth Park had served as the model for Spanish Moss Park, which the protagonist Danny Blue enters as a deadly storm is approaching:

Even through the rain and cloud-filled dark of the approaching storm, and through the shadow of the valley of dread spreading wide inside him, Danny Blue could see clearly enough the gargantuan tree that spanned a good seventy-five feet around and stood the height of a three-story house. The size of the oak would have been less astounding had he been looking at the entire tree. As it was, what stood before him was what had been left after all of the tree's upper branches had been sawed off and only the huge stubs of four or five main branches remained.

The grandeur of the trees lined along the promenade reaching from the southern to northern ends of the park lent the area an aura of solemnity and sacred spaciousness that surpassed its historical identification as a major Civil War campsite for Confederate soldiers. It was also, ironically, the same park where a century after the Civil War my mother, as family legend had it, made her brood of children stand up to racist Whites who said they had no right to play there as their children were doing.

Crossing Abercorn and then Drayton, I saw a line of people standing outside the Sentient Bean Coffee Shop next to Brighter Day Health Food Store. They must have power from a generator, I thought. Good for them. But aside from those clustered outside the coffee shop, quite a few people were also milling about walking dogs and sharing stories of how they made it through the storm. The day after Floyd had bypassed the city, the only people I saw anywhere were first responders on patrol. This time around, the recommended evacuation as opposed to a mandatory one had clearly encouraged a greater number to stay.

A short distance away was the top of the Confederate Monument still standing above a large moss-draped oak tree fallen a few yards east of the statue, and another smaller tree on the southern walkway. I hurried toward the larger oak, as if it were going to suddenly stand up and run away, and began taking photos of it with the monument in the background. Similar scenes greeted me throughout the park. While the famous fountain (with its classic sculptures of triton mermen and swans) in its center appeared not to have been damaged by flying debris, the various surrounding paths and side lawns leading to the fountain were all littered green with fallen branches and broken plants. How different it was from that beautiful sunny day in May 2010 when I stood with historian Barry Sheehy, photographer Cindy Wallace, and historian Vaughnette Goode-Walker to take photographs for the *Civil War Savannah* book series website. Moreover, only a few days before, the water of the fountain had been dyed purple in recognition of October as Domestic Violence Awareness Month.

Likewise, many of the trees uprooted and thrown to the ground had been adorned with bright purple ribbons and the image of their sprawled bodies reinforced the message of how violence slaughtered peace in an extremely disturbing way. There was no question that we all needed to come to terms with the unforgivable reality of domestic brutalities that marred the existence of far too many women, men, and children. Nor was there any question that we still needed to confront humanity's reliance on vehemence in general when it came to trying to resolve disagreements over anything from how to place toilet paper on a spool, to whether or not girls around the world should receive the same opportunities for education as boys.

If man-made global warming truly was the cause of so many trees' deaths, then it had been a case of murder by violence in the guise of apathy. And apathy had proven no less deadly than exploding IEDs in Afghanistan, drones in Iraq, assault weapons on the streets of Chicago or Los Angeles, clashes between cartels in Mexico, rapes and kidnappings in Nigeria, terrorism in Paris or Orlando, policemen's bullets erasing black people's lives, and hatred in the hearts of all who were unable to abide the presence of anyone perceived to be remotely different from themselves. They had all, in their dedication to worshipping violence, left behind scores of hacked bodies and rivers of coagulating blood. Whereas one could consider human-initiated life-annihilating violence as a natural by-product of history, one could also view it as a choice indicating a certain kind of insanity of which we needed to heal ourselves.

The agony human beings inflicted upon human beings was bad enough; the idea that our absurd ways were somehow driving nature insane made a scary very visual kind of sense walking through the aftermath of Matthew's visit. One corner of the area near the Forsyth Park Café looked more like the Okefenokee Swamp than a favorite place for tossing Frisbees. In another, not far west of the fountain, I gasped to see how a palm tree had fallen onto the outstretched branch of a magnolia like a lover or a soldier dying in someone's trembling arms.

Near Drayton and Gaston Streets at the northeast corner of the park, a green toppled sign surrounded by a broken street lamp and fallen limbs read: "SCAD Welcome Ctr. Downtown Attractions Visitor Center." An arrow at the end of the text pointed to the sky. Around the trunk of the tree still standing next to it was a shiny purple ribbon and cordoning off the entire section was a long red tape. On the corner of the intersection across the street, another tree had fallen between a sign identifying the Savannah Law School and traffic signs cautioning drivers to beware of crossing pedestrians. The body of yet another palm tree lay stretched out as I walked back toward the northern Bull Street entrance to Forsyth Park.

From there, I strolled past more green corpses next to the Mercer-Williams House, extended across Monterey Square, shattered to splinters in Madison Square, Chippewa Square, on past Wright Square. Between Broughton Street and Johnson Square an alarm began to ring nonstop and sirens started wailing a block away. Reaching City Hall on Bay Street, I started down the gray stone steps beside it. Then, walking upon the sloping surface of Factor's Walk with its cobbled stones laid by slaves—my African ancestors—I was not sure what to expect upon turning the corner onto River Street. Would I see broken storefronts, dead birds scattered everywhere, or boats tossed onto the docks? Would I see the Eugene Talmadge Memorial Bridge, which I hoped would soon be renamed The Tomochichi-Oglethorpe Bridge, collapsed beneath the weight of an insufferable racial injustice which neither history nor hurricanes could endure any longer?

There were, in fact, from where I stood, no catastrophic sights to behold. The African-American Family Monument continued to stand as it had for the past fourteen years (since July 27, 2002) and the river flowed on just as it had been doing since long before there was a city called Savannah. To my right, next to the city hall docking ramp for the Savannah Belles Ferry water transport system, a colony of three or four seagulls landed and turned their heads toward the bridge while simultaneously seeming to wait for someone to throw a few crumbs their way. To my left, a flock of pigeons settled on the red bricks and moved expectantly back and forth. Where had these birds found shelter during the worst hours of the tempest? Look at us, I thought, survivors all gathered here together the morning after the fury. Across the river, on Hutchinson Island, a long line of still-standing forestry swayed beneath the persistent press of a gust of wind.

Owens-Thomas House in Savannah, Georgia by Aberjhani.

Dreams of the Immortal City

"The sellers certainly didn't want to be enslaved: the purchased often committed suicide to avoid it. So how did it work?"

—Toni Morrison (*The Origin of Others*)

Dreams have been a defining element of my life for as long as I can remember. As a child, I was prone to daydreaming in school and instead of dutifully copying onto my paper the numbers or alphabets written in white chalk on the blackboard, I often drew labyrinth-like structures filled with wandering eyes, miniature suns, expanding spirals, and clusters of diamonds. These lead-pencil masterpieces did not signal to my grade-school teachers at Spencer Elementary—as such behavior might to a modern educator— that I was artistically inclined. Mostly, it seemed to make them wonder about my sanity each time they popped the bubble of my daydream and then looked back and forth from a startled gaze to the mystery of my drawings. Sometimes I have wondered if any of them ever reached a point where they recognized obvious parallels, or even thread-slight similarities, between my doodles back then and works later on by certain modern abstract or expressionist artists.

As an adult, my dreams took on the kind of meanings and qualities they do in many people's lives. They became synonymous with the word "goals," as in dreams of a future authoring books of such stupendous appeal that readers marched in protest against any stores that allowed stocks of my titles to run out. They also at times reflected an uncanny predilection for retro-cognition and precognition, re-illuminating events from my past to provide insights I had not known I needed; and, offering tantalizing glimpses of things yet to come. This latter quality, I learned, was one that ran in the family. Puffing on her favorite pipe, Grandmother Elsie informed me one day that, "When I was a girl, God showed me a whole lot of things I didn't really understand. Then as the years went by, I saw all those things come to pass one by one. And then I understood."

Not long after returning to Savannah from a tour of duty with the U.S. Air Force in England, I joined an Edgar Cayce dream study group. We met at the former Stardust Book Emporium located downtown in the Historic District on York Street, only a few yards away from Wright Square where slave auctions used to be held the first Tuesday of every month. About ten of us met once a week to share any dreams we wanted the group to discuss, often applying Jungian or Caycean interpretations to them. I suppose I was the nerd in the group because it was not enough for me to simply describe my dreams. I had to type them up, make copies, and pass them out so that as I read aloud everyone else could silently read along and meditate more deeply on any crucial detail or nuance before sharing their thoughts.

It was about this time, around 1989, that I experienced one of the most puzzling dream-visions I had ever had: in the dream, I was engaged in some form of guerilla warfare in downtown Savannah. Along with four others, I ran from the corner of one building to another while dodging the bullets of our enemies. Although I was part of a team, we were all on different corners some distance apart but able to signal each other so we could move in unison. Despite the fact that we were engaged in a war, none of those on my side seemed to have any kind of weapons. At one point, we simultaneously looked up and flew into the sky. Hovering in the air, we first formed a line above the city and stretched out our arms. Then, suddenly, a bolt of energy sprang from one of our outstretched hands and jumped from one person to the next. When the energy bolt reached the last person, it expanded into a giant grid, somewhat like an enormous net of light, or the frame of a geodesic dome that covered Savannah. While this happened, others continued to shoot at us from the ground. An unexpected shift of some kind occurred on the ground and in the air, and spirits then began to rise up out of the earth. At first there seemed to be hundreds, and then thousands. They rose up into the air and flew straight through the net of light we had created. Once through the net, they would disappear in a flash. The dream ended with lights blazing all over the city like New Year's Eve fireworks.

One of the interpretations offered by my study group for this dream was that it may have been a metaphorical narrative describing a situation in which I had felt alone but then discovered I was not, that I in fact had friends willing to lend assistance when or if they could. Another interpretation was that I had felt trapped by the circumstances of my life—since it had been my physical-world intention to return to Europe or the American west coast rather than settle in Savannah— but then made my peace with those circumstances by opening myself up to other possibilities and potential opportunities. The different interpretations made sense enough but the problem was I could not find a way to apply them to a concrete enough situation or event in my life at the time. Which was something I usually could do within a week or so after experiencing such a dream-vision. So I decided it must be a reference to something which had not happened yet but which would likely happen soon. Only that was not how it went either. Weeks and months passed without the occurrence of anything that felt like a manifestation of the dream I'd had.

I began to take note, when going downtown in the evenings to participate in open mic poetry recitals, of tour guides offering "ghost tours" and would recall the spirits in the dream rising up from the earth. As the years passed, with the increasing popularity of books like Margaret Wayt DeBolt's classic *Savannah Spectres*, the city staked claim to a reputation as "America's most haunted city." As a result, a variety of ghost tours developed to scare visitors with tales of restless souls wandering about the Historic District or staring out dusty second-floor windows. Could the growth of this niche market have been my dream's elusive message? For the most part, eventually I stopped thinking about it. But every now and then some unexpected spark of light would bring it to mind for a moment or so.

II.

Flash forward some two decades later to December 2009 and I am much less interested in dreams than I am in wading through the tsunami of economic woes which has engulfed almost every industrial nation on the planet. Like many caregivers who spend years devoting their life's energies and resources to the well-being of another, once I had completed the task caring for my mother and she had claimed her well-earned rest in peace, I found myself in the position of having to rebuild my own life. That meant producing one book after another in attempts to simultaneously increase the catalogue of my works and cultivate the audience with which I had been unable to interact during the years of caregiving.

When a literary agent contacted me regarding the possibility of writing a biography on a major figure of the Harlem Renaissance, I started exploring the prospect by compiling notes to create a synopsis for the proposed title. The lightning bolt of opportunity then struck a second time as the representative for a forthcoming book series on Civil War Savannah asked to meet with me. My first response was, "I don't really write about the Civil War. My work is closer to the Harlem Renaissance and contemporary culture where black folks have a lot more say-so about the issues affecting the lives they're living."

"I know," she answered. "We want to talk about hiring you to edit the books."

Well, could she possibly have said anything more unexpected than that? The notion intrigued me deeply because dealing with Civil War Savannah would mean dealing with slavery in Savannah, something as politely ignored by most natives of the city as clotted mucus on a smiling senator's mustache. It was possible I knew a little more about the subject than the average Savannah native. In May 2006, *Connect Savannah* news weekly had published my article (please see appendix D) about anthropologist Deborah L. Mack's work to spearhead in the city a "reinterpretation" of urban slavery that would require official tour guides to increase their knowledge about individual slaves who had lived in the Historic District.

The most that I knew about it was what Whittington B. Johnson had traveled all the way from Miami to research and then publish in his eye-opening book, *Black Savannah 1788-1864*. It was due to Johnson's efforts that I—and numerous others—first learned there had been such a thing as black slave owners, so I was a little less shocked than some when author Edward P. Jones turned that funky twist of historical fate into his Pulitzer Prize-winning novel, *The Known World*. I had also had occasional conversations with Rev. Charles Lwanga Hoskins, a retired cleric who developed a passion for researching Savannah's black past and self-published several books on the subject.

Dr. Mack had come to Savannah from Chicago. Reverend Hoskins had been transplanted to the city from Trinidad by way of New Jersey, and Wittington B. Johnson from Florida. It had long been a bone of contention for me that in a city where African Americans made up more than fifty percent of the population, people were always coming from somewhere else to speak our truth and tell our stories while we seemed to place so little value on who or what we were in the global, cultural, or historical scheme of things. This caused me much serious silent grief. Forced to consider the hypocrisy of criticizing others who declined to act to prevent the erasure of major chapters from our history if I walked away from the challenge of editing important volumes on Savannah during the Civil War, I thought longer and harder about the challenge it presented.

Whereas the job could help relax some of my financial anxiety, it could also do a lot more. With the approaching 2011 sesquicentennial of the Civil War, the proposed series could remind the world that in the end things never turned out well for those who insisted on depriving people of even an illusion of self-ownership or dignity. Humanity had learned this lesson many times over and yet certain members of the species refused to evolve past it. Personal status and entire kingdoms had been lost to seemingly bottomless desires for wealth, sex, drugs, power, or, strangely enough, powerlessness, extracted from conditions forced upon peoples' lives. This focus on the deprivation of human beings' will and ability to act freely on their own behalf was trained so intensely in one direction that it led to blindness toward others. Inevitably, repeatedly, it destroyed or at best delayed the realization of a potentially magnificent destiny.

The vampiric impulse nevertheless persisted. While condemnation may have been universal to an extent, so was the gleeful acceptance of predators who engaged what they considered the benefits of: forced labor, debt bondage, forced marriages, child prostitution, forced begging, child soldiers, forced criminality, involuntary servitude, forced pregnancies to sell newborn infants, exploitation of men, women, and children displaced by war or natural disasters, and imprisonment of African-Americans, Latinos, and impoverished Whites to drive the profits of a private prison-construction industry.

How was it possible that as late as the year 2000 the United Nations would find itself passing the "Protocol to Prevent, Suppress, and Punish Trafficking in Persons as part of the Convention against Transnational Organised Crime?" How was it that five years later the International Labor Organization would prove just how desperately the protocol was needed when it released its first *Global Report on Forced Labour* and proclaimed that 12.3 million people across the globe were living in some form of modern slavery? Presumably many more would have been identified if the UN's extended definition of human trafficking had been applied:

"Trafficking in persons" shall mean the recruitment, transportation, transfer, harbouring or receipt of persons, by means of the threat or use of force or other forms of coercion, of abduction,

of fraud, of deception, of the abuse of power or of a position of vulnerability or of the giving or receiving of payments or benefits to achieve the consent of a person having control over another person, for the purpose of exploitation. Exploitation shall include, at a minimum, the exploitation of the prostitution of others or other forms of sexual exploitation, forced labour or services, slavery or practices similar to slavery, servitude or the removal of organs..."

Despite major differences between slavery as it is known in the 21st century and human bondage as it was practiced during the years of the Transatlantic Slave Trade, with its stops in Europe, South America, the Caribbean, and North America, the latter type of slavery remains the original model for the UN's discombobulating definition. Savannah had been a major destination for the importation of slaves right up until the Civil War and even as I contemplated working with historians about human trafficking in the city's past, there were no reasons to assume all the various ladies and gentlemen of the night peddling their flesh throughout the city were doing so because they had always dreamed of selling their bodies to strangers. Some were there in a continuation of the long-recognized historical forms coercion. Others were there because of the more subtle forms of mental manipulations, economic deprivation, and circumstances of social status rarely recognized as brands of slavery.

III.

I had grown up in the shadows of forced servitude's artifacts and walked among its remnants but never confronted or made any kind of conscious personal peace with it. The Confederate Monument in Forsyth Park held no significance for me when hurrying past it as a child largely because the park at that time was not a place where Blacks were likely to hang out. But also because while growing up I had never heard anyone talk about slavery in Savannah, or its subsequent lingering impact on the cultural mindset.

During Black History Month in high school, any allusions to slavery were made in the context of American slavery in general and never with reference to the once-thriving industry within my hometown. Yet there were silent codes of Jim Crow conduct which were direct extensions of slave and slave-master mentalities. A black individual still automatically stepped to the side when moving toward a white person on a sidewalk too narrow to accommodate both. A combination of blackness and poverty meant one should act doubly-humble before a white of any social or economic status whatsoever. With the right to vote, occupy any seat on a public bus on a first-come-first-served basis, and shop in any downtown store where U.S. currency was accepted, African Americans were expected to, and did, ignore any less ostensible forms of oppression.

As an adult, I had lived in the Historic District in a basement apartment on Gordon's Row where I swore I sometimes felt the ghosts of slaves moving as quietly as they could toward the Savannah River. And also as an adult I had, in fact, stood on the Stoddard Ranges above the barracoons (McCluskey's Vaults) next to River Street where slaves were rumored (falsely as it turned out) to have been penned up like hogs, and there felt those presences along with certain others while reciting poetry before an audience in the open air. *Why, I wondered with every movement or murmur felt, are you still here? Why haven't you moved on after all these years?*

Could it be the time had come to find out? Many people thought so. Yet what were they to make of ongoing practices of denial that sustained cultures of racism, sexism, classism, and other thinly-veiled types of oppression. How, for example, was it possible that year after year debates were held over the appropriateness or inappropriateness of naming the bridge stretching across the Savannah River after an avowed white supremacist? Was the dismissal of such an insult to African Americans and democracy a kind of enslavement to apathy? To willful ignorance? Fear? When looked at through different lens of psychology, it added up to a form of mental bondage which many visitors and transplants to Savannah quickly recognized but about which the indigenous black population seemed oddly unaware. Therefore, the discussion I was preparing to have about war and slavery in the city not only concerned the history already behind us. It was also about the history we were living at that moment.

In my meeting with author Barry Sheehy, photographer Cindy Wallace, and historian Vaughnette Goode-Walker, I listened as they spoke about the work they had been doing for half a decade to create the series that would become *Civil War Savannah*. I understood that Sheehy and Wallace for several years had quietly gone around Savannah's Historic District and surrounding areas taking photographs of buildings and land areas—as in the remnants of battle fields—directly linked to the Civil War. This photographic documentation began very naturally to evolve into an idea for a book. Goode-Walker had been involved in research for the Telfair Museum of Art's Owens-Thomas House and founded independently the *Footprints of Savannah Walking Tour*. Her addition to the documentation project was a natural one. The idea for one book developed further into an idea for a series of books.

Sitting at a table in the J Christopher restaurant downtown on Liberty Street, they showed me a thick notebook-bound manuscript for book one of the proposed series and a thinner wire-bound manuscript for book two. As we continued to speak, I casually flipped through the pages of the first volume. They were filled with images of buildings and monuments I had seen and walked past much of my life. Without warning, they inserted themselves into my mind in a new, raw, and spectacular way. There was something as terrifyingly profane as it was amazingly sacred about the fact that we were within walking distance of still-existing squares and buildings where black people had been routinely sold and where northern liberators had set up headquarters to wage battle on behalf the Union.

I listened as the authors of this work-in-progress explained their intent to commemorate the sesquicentennial of the American Civil War by shining a broader, brighter beam of light on an aspect of the past few at the time ever addressed in any significant way. These documentarians were not interested in re-telling the story of the Civil War as so many had already capably done. They wanted to capture as best they could the very fine nuances of the magic of history that had allowed Savannah to survive the war largely intact, providing the world with a kind of living time capsule where visitors could still walk in the footsteps and even enter some of the homes of people for whom slavery had been the "norm."

They wanted to illustrate, if such a thing were possible, the mindset, daily activities, financial expectations and financial realities that made slavery a functional institution. In other words, how did ordinary human beings, ministers, bankers, architects, brokers, journalists, store owners, saloon managers, teachers, and even slaves themselves, maintain a system of existence destined for universal condemnation and rejection? The books would also serve to promote the historic preservation movement that had done so much to make Savannah what it remains in modern times: a rare kind of living museum filled with breath-taking cultural wonders. And all of this they hoped to accomplish, not very realistically I thought, within a year from the time of our meeting.

Of those at the table, only Goode-Walker (who previously had contributed an article to the Harlem Renaissance encyclopedia project) was a native Savannahian and black like me. Sheehy was Canadian and Wallace from Texas. The sincerity of their intent to render the city of Savannah and the pages of Civil War history a worthy service was evident from the exceptional quality of the work – which was apparent even though the manuscript was still in late stages of development. Moreover, their passion for the subject of my hometown had inspired them to actually put in the time, commit available resources, and perform the labor required to accomplish a feat that could only be described as monumental. Twin imps of envy and guilt nibbled away at my ego as I turned to Goode-Walker and said loud enough for everyone to hear, "We should have done this."

It was a strange outburst to make because she in fact was already part of a "we" who were "doing this." And "we" had all met so they might consider inviting me to join their team in the capacity of an editor. Sometime later on, I would conclude that for the purpose of telling their specific chosen story, those involved actually represented an ideal balance of cosmopolitan objectivity and homegrown authenticity. Anything less would likely have run the risk of profiling the city and its people in terms of exotic otherness, or of wallowing in residual grievances that made for good historical drama but not for good truth-telling. The story of the American Civil War is essentially one of human beings— Northerners, Southerners, Blacks, Whites, men, women— holding themselves accountable for the future of a nation. Some did so with informed ideas about what their individual choices could or would mean: others did so with little awareness of, or at least little regard for, the larger moral, economic, or political implications.

One of the biggest questions I had to ask myself while considering working on the series was whether or not I would be able to remain sufficiently objective. You might think it would not be a problem for someone trained as a journalist and living in an era that saw the Berlin Wall come tumbling down while Nelson Mandela stepped up into the presidency of South Africa. But ancestral memory can be a strange thing which at times feels more like ancestral empathy. Many African Americans have had some sense of this when watching films like *Roots* or *Amistad*, just as Jews have felt the same watching *Schindler's List* or reading *Sophie's Choice*. They know the situation does not apply to them directly yet experience moments of personal identification so deeply that they are swallowed whole for entire days by pain, or fear, or rage until reminding themselves that they are reacting to something from the past and far removed from their current lives. It is not, perhaps, unlike what some people experience when hypnotized to revisit a traumatic event and become so emotionally immersed in the ordeal they respond as if physically involved in it.

I reminded myself that I had had doubts about working on *Encyclopedia of the Harlem Renaissance* as well. In addition, the more I looked through the manuscripts the more clear it became that fine-tuning such an epically-scaled work within the established timeframe would require the input of several editors rather than one. As our meeting ended, I agreed to take volume two of the series home with me and promised to read through it more thoroughly to determine if I could be of any significant service to the project.

Once home, I started reading and, out of a habit developed over years of working with my and other authors' manuscripts, picked up a pencil to begin making notes. The cover of the working manuscript featured a gallery of images that included the black educator Susie King Taylor, black minister Ulysses Houston, slave broker George Wylly, slave trader Charles A.L. Lamar, and broker W.C. Dawson. The eyes of each seemed to say, "You think you know me but you don't." They were right. Once I started, it became impossible to imagine not contributing my best efforts to the series.

Going through the pages I had received from Sheehy, his narrative struck me as both necessarily detached and passionately intimate. The kind of balance many found difficult to strike. It not only took readers into the hidden back rooms of buildings where slaves had been sold and through doorways I had passed through while out for a carefree stroll or night on the town, but inside the passageways of his subjects' minds and hearts.

Their delusions are so sincere, I thought as I reviewed the stories of trauma-survivor Lamar trying to inflict devastation upon the lives of Africans by struggling to re-open the slave trade; and Louis Manigault, who was genuinely surprised to realize his former slaves did not love him anywhere nearly as much as he had believed. I reconsidered the lives of slaves like "Jane," who could not make peace with slavery in any form and therefore constantly looked for ways to escape. Even more compelling was that of Susie King Taylor. One of those historic figures seemingly able to take slavery in stride, she rose above any debilitating personal impact it may have had to create a permanent record of the institution in its final days and provide an important portrait of African Americans' transition from bondage to freedom.

Two days after meeting with the CWS team, I was invited to submit a contract proposal I presumed would be considered along with any others submitted for the job of editing the work. Several days later, I was hired for the job and my 150-years-long journey back into Savannah's past began in earnest. Strangely enough, just as I had had to purchase a new computer almost a decade earlier to complete *Encyclopedia of the Harlem Renaissance*, I had to do the same in order to accommodate Cindy Wallace's brilliant but huge image files for *Civil War Savannah*. The 750 megabytes of memory on my computer had been considered substantial when I bought it and resources on the Internet had allowed me to work around any need to invest in another one. But the combined photos, text, and programs required to compose just the first volume of the series took up almost an entire gigabyte. To me, this provided even further proof of the blood, sweat, and tears that had gone into the work and pushed me to equip myself with the proper digital tools to get the job done.

The original plan was to publish volumes one and two of the series simultaneously and we hoped to debut both in February 2011. Eventually, our publisher told us this would not be possible. But before settling into that reality, I moved back and forth between work on both books as if traveling between time and space to acclimate my senses to a world as alien as one could get and yet remain, somehow, as agonizingly familiar as the scars on a whipped slave's body.

After steeling myself to exercise unfailing editorial objectivity when it came to dealing with the stories of secessionists so hell-bent on retaining slavery that they were willing to see their sons, brothers, and husbands go off and die for it, I was stunned by aspects of their narratives which revealed more about their humanity than about the wrongs or rights of slavery itself. Until then, I had generally accepted the assumption that any sense of humanity was inapplicable to those who had enslaved my ancestors.

The problem, of course, had always been the uneasy awareness that Africans had also enslaved and sold Africans. There had been a qualitative difference where motives and conduct towards the slaves was concerned but the definitive element of depriving individuals of their freedom had been the same. Moreover, as W.E.B. Du Bois and many others since have pointed out, because American Whites did not invent slavery, they were simply, from 1619 until 1865, among the latest in history to convince themselves it was a divinely-sanctioned solution to a growing demand for labor within a rapidly-expanding country. Nevertheless, as Du Bois also noted: "So long as slavery was a matter of race and color, it made the conscience of the nation uneasy and continually affronted its ideals."

The racist presumption that Africans were devoid of any true humanity prompted within me a corresponding conviction that those acting on such a belief most likely were the least human of us all. Prior to leaving Savannah to attend college, encounters with progressive-minded Whites had been too few to convince me otherwise. And while I was able to drop the racially-charged fears, anger, and suspicions of my childhood upon my return to the city, I continued to experience enough inter-racial and intra-racial prejudice to realize my hometown, like my homeland, still had a great deal of work to do. For one very important thing, somebody needed to figure out why so many ghosts insisted on hanging around the city and then do something about it.

IV.

Savannah was every bit as haunted as the tour guides who liked to dress up in vintage period costumes proclaimed it was. But did they really understand what was haunting our city or why? Many of them took their scripts from my now-deceased friend Margaret Wayt DeBolt, who pointed out: "From restored townhouses on the historic squares, when a genteel presence might come with the lease, to newer homes on the sites of old plantations and battlefields, each has its story. So do the forts, house museums and restored waterfront of Georgia's first city, which has survived pirates, wars, two military occupations, fires, epidemics, and tourist popularity after decades of genteel 'too poor to paint, too proud to whitewash' poverty." (Savannah Spectres, p.1)

Stories of Telfair Museum benefactress Mary Telfair's watchful gaze causing furniture to move, runaway slaves still attempting escape in the 1990s from chains left behind in the 1850s, and Confederate soldiers who appeared suddenly in doorways all made very entertaining tales while sidestepping a stalled confrontation with the more flesh-and-bone-endowed reality.

The more I labored in the data-rich mines of the past the more I allowed myself to acknowledge something which must have shadowed my thoughts all my life: Savannah was not haunted just by slavery, but by the precise role it had played in slavery's long existence on the North American continent, by the struggle most of its citizens waged to preserve the peculiar institution. It was a given every Black History Month that someone would talk about local historic African-American figures like Mother Matilda Taylor Beasley, W.W. Law, and Hosea Williams. What you did not hear about was how or why the names of main streets like LaRoche Avenue came to be named after white human beings who bought and sold black human beings. And it was, as well, excruciatingly, grievously, haunted by the price it had paid in the form of the lives of its sons, brothers, fathers, and husbands for efforts to sustain a system history had already proven unsustainable many times over.

Releasing the scalding guilt and cutting shame of horrors inflicted upon another is much easier than relinquishing those inflicted upon oneself. The city's collective conscience could follow previous examples in history and forgive the atrocities of actual slavery committed against slaves themselves. But what was it to do with the knowledge that children completely unaware of the greater ramifications of slavery were led to the Civil War slaughter in its name? How does one acknowledge with forgiveness such an unforgiving mutilation of one's own mind, body, soul, and legacy?

Indeed: how many family members, though still alive in the physical sense had sat like phantoms in the ghostly sense, for years talking about the cousin, uncle, or nephew they lost in the "War of Northern Aggression?" How many women died clutching letters from men they had planned to marry just after the war but never did because the men never returned? How many disembodied souls have kneeled beside a loved one and reached out to comfort them only to discover they could not because they themselves no longer breathed air?

Human nature is a complex formulation of spiritual ambiguities and biological urgencies we strive to mold into meaningful experiences which, collectively, are then referred to as: Life. Such, at least, was my conclusion the more deeply I traveled into the pages of *Savannah, Immortal City*, and then *Bankers, Brokers, and Bay Lane—Inside the Slave Trade*. The anger, fear, and resentment simmering within my own human nature began to subside and I allowed myself to accept the individual human complexities of those to whom I had denied them for so long.

A powerful turning point came when reviewing the story of Father Peter Whelan, who was far more interested in tending to wounded bodies and souls than he was in upholding a political ideology of any kind. Dressed in tattered clothing while enduring frigid weather and the diseased environments of POW camps, he focused the whole of his life's energies on alleviating the suffering of those wounded and imprisoned during the war, even when he was the one suffering and, for all intended purposes, imprisoned. What mattered to Whelan "was to allay misery and gain souls for God," and he clearly considered himself expendable in the fulfillment of such a demanding mission.

Emotionally, even more compelling for me was the story of a different kind of father, that of Berrien Zettler's. At the age of sixty-four, after learning his son had been wounded in Virginia, the patriarch traveled by every available means, including walking more than fifty miles, to find his son and bring him home to recuperate. As Confederate soldiers often did, the younger Zettler chose to remain on active duty rather than accept a disability discharge and he not only lived to engage his enemy at least once more but also to share his tale with the world in a memoir. The son's gung-ho bravado and dedication to assigned duty was one thing, but what moved me was a father's love so intensely unwavering that it gave him the courage and strength to traverse terrains splattered with body parts and booming with the sounds of warfare to save his own. That was not a Southern idealist's commitment to the Confederate cause. It was a human being's determination to protect someone he loved at any and all costs.

Stories like Zettler's and Father Whelan's provided the missing counterparts to classic slave narratives I had read as a teenager. The number of Whites who had died fighting for a mission they did not necessarily champion may not have been as numerous or heartbreaking as the number of the Blacks who over centuries had been ripped from the womb of their native land and forced to breed generations of slaves, but it was just as maliciously absurd and tragically misguided. In fact, the entire spectacle of the war, on both sides of the Mason Dixon line, appeared to me to have been glued together as much by crippling ignorance and clownish arrogance as it had been by exemplary courage and redemptive heroism.

While working on the manuscript pages, lost and fallen souls seemed one by one to filter themselves between the lines of sentences, rise up in front of me, this one white, that one black, a woman, a child, an elderly soul with a shredded heart, give a bewildered solemn nod, and then float upward beyond my gaze. That was when it occurred: the dream I had experienced twenty years before came back. But this time it happened with my eyes as wide open as a cloudless sky. Here were the souls I had seen rising up out of the earth and propelling themselves through a net of light that spanned the sky across Savannah while I stood with several others in the air and watched them break free of the shackles of history and the denial of verity that had bound them for centuries.

Written in one of my notebooks were these words attributed to the great Sufi teacher and poet Rumi: "There is nothing more noble than the manifestation of a noble vision or prophecy." I felt a lot of what I believed he meant by the statement, but mostly I felt stunned these bewildered souls had had to wait so long for this act of literary shamanism to set them free. Why had we been so determined to hold on to our hidden agonies instead of releasing them into the air and light of acknowledgment where they could finally heal? Instead of allowing ourselves to learn from the past we had denied its brutal reality and that denial had simply sustained, although deeply hidden and guarded, the unceasing misery of the original now 150-year-old wound.

The more I worked on the pages of *Savannah, Immortal City*, and *Brokers, Bankers, and Bay Lane-Inside the Slave Trade*, the more I realized the labor truly was a kind of not-so-gentle exorcism that might cause many of those who read the books to cringe with inherited guilt and shame but which would at long last allow unseen others to put down their sabers and guns, and enter whatever fields of light or shadow awaited them. Possibly it also articulated the reason the city had not allowed me to permanently relocate elsewhere following my mother's death, a time when I was certain I was supposed to do precisely that. Maybe it had not happened because I had not fully understood what it meant to call Savannah my home, what it meant to witness the dark flight of wounded souls from gilded burial grounds of repressed memory to higher planes of freedom.

Now, I understood it was not just the vanished house where I had been born or the government project of Hitch Village (please see appendix E) where I had spent most of my childhood years and which had also been demolished. Nor was it just the poverty which had kept my youth such intimate company or the racial disparities that had made my mother's and father's lives such challenging ones. That was the Savannah with which my soul was most familiar so it had worked its way into a number of poems, stories, and essays. The Savannah I had to wait to discover was and is a city which remains emblematic of the United States of America itself: a city at the time of the 150th anniversary of the Civil War so intent on denying the horrors of its past it could not free itself long enough to embrace the potential triumphs of its future. Nevertheless, both the living and the dead were due their peace where this particular issue of a self-inflicted holocaust was concerned and the time had come to let them claim it.

Whereas other cities around the country hosted major symposiums, reenactments, and other program observances to acknowledge the 150th anniversary of the Civil War and associated events, few people outside of those affiliated with special interest groups were aware of any such activities in Savannah. Consequently, the publication of the first volume of *Civil War Savannah* in 2011 and the second in 2012 with lectures and photography exhibitions by the authors came to represent two of the region's most significant commemorations of both the war itself and the *Emancipation Proclamation.*

Is it possible city officials and general citizens alike did not push for any extravaganza-styled productions because everyone had begun to sense that even as one dream of freedom had been realized, they were only just beginning to understand the full depths of a more recent increasing terror?

V.

Chapter thirteen of *Brokers, Bankers, and Bay Lane—Inside the Slave Trade,* tells the story of would-be businessman and political provocateur Charles A. Lamar's attempt to reopen the Atlantic Slave Trade in 1858, long after it had been outlawed in 1807. With a gang of like-minded plotters, including apparently Africans who believed in using slavery to their own benefit, Lamar successfully, albeit illegally, imported some 420 African slaves on a vessel known as the *Wanderer*. He and co-conspirators went to trial for the offense but were declared not guilty. In addition to whatever monetary benefits he may have gained from the crime, Lamar's action helped stir dormant public debates over the institution of slavery itself and contributed to the intense division between northern and southern states which eventually led to war. He profited from the conflict by manufacturing rifles for the Confederate army and by operating a blockage-running export and import business.

There was no reason to be shocked by the predatory instincts that directed Lamar's behavior. Worse heinous conduct, such as humans feasting upon the flesh of humans, has been recorded. However, given the perspective history has provided on some members of humanity's addiction to slavery since Lamar worked so earnestly to reopen the Atlantic slave trade, there should have been enough shock, awe, and outrage in September 2013 to bring every form of business-as-usual to a prolonged halt in Savannah. Except it did not. It was then that the U.S. Attorney's Office announced the results of *Operation Dark Night*, an extensive investigation which revealed a sex trafficking ring operating on the southside of Savannah. Periodically relocating to Florida, South Carolina, and North Carolina, the ring reportedly originated in Mexico where women from there, Nicaragua, and other locations were promised assistance in their pursuit of the American dream. They ended up instead serving against their will as objects of sexual pleasure, being forced to commit various acts as much as 30 times a day.

The Savannah-Chatham Metropolitan Police Department, the Chatham County Sheriff's Office, the Garden City Police Department, and the Chatham-Savannah Counter Narcotics Team joined forces with Homeland Security Investigations, the FBI, the Bureau of Alcohol, Tobacco, Firearms, and Explosives, the U.S. Customs and Border Protection (CBP), the CBP Air and Marine Operations, and the Internal Revenue Service's Criminal Investigations to execute *Operation Dark*

Night. What was touted as "the largest sex trafficking investigation ever prosecuted in the Southern District of Georgia" resulted in the rescue of eleven victims and the arrest of forty so-called "Johns." The scope of the strategy and magnitude of the results provided reason to believe law enforcement officials were beginning to have a corrective impact on an infestation of slavery as heinous as that in the 1700s. However, two years later, in October 2015, ongoing investigations netted additional arrests for adult and child trafficking in Savannah and nearby Pooler. The nation's and the world's human trafficking dilemma remained as horrendous in the region as anywhere else.

It is possible that the increasing growth of the hotel industry in the city, heavy tourism, restaurant culture, strategic geographic location, and accepted above-average poverty level make it easier for offenders to conceal their activities and therefore make the region particularly susceptible to the crime. Or: is it more likely that the same disregard for any sense of innate sanctity regarding individual human lives that prompted generations of Southerners to place their faith in a doomed system is something we have yet to evolve beyond as a species? Why would that be the case?

Perhaps slavery in its myriad forms is only one manifestation of humanity's belief in violence as a solution to various personal, domestic, community, national, and international conundrums. Or maybe slavery has been with us for centuries because of the inclination to maintain economic systems geared more toward commodifying human existence than developing its spiritual, creative, or scientific potentials. Such commodification instantly erases any recognition of humanity as a priceless value unto itself and reduces individuals as well as entire races, or a specific gender, to a bargain-priced "other." The practice of receiving compensation for your cooperative commodification is less soothing than many would prefer in a world where one person, or a small group of people, can not only purchase and manipulate industries but also the laws that govern them. Whereas commodification of human existence itself is not by definition slavery, it may be argued that it provides the framework which makes slavery both possible and desirable.

Slavery stands as a cruel obliteration of consideration for any value an individual might place upon her or his self-identified dreams. This remains true whether it is viewed: as a necessary source of labor to sustain economic or institutional growth, as a political mechanism for ridding a society of unwanted misfits, as just punishment for humans who have committed certain crimes, as a means to satisfy undisciplined lust, or as one appropriate outcome of war. If freedom is nothing else, it is not only the legal and inherent right to pursue one's self-defined vision of happiness without intent to cause another grievous harm, but the ability to do so. In Savannah as elsewhere, new challenges to that pursuit have arisen in ways no one expected.

The realization of dreams, like every battle for freedom, has always required compromise to one degree or another. When the result of a concession, however, is the mutilation of your soul or the cancellation of someone else's future, then it may be said the desired goal was corrupted or destroyed rather than attained. My initial dream of "the immortal city" revealed the work which had to be completed before any number of individuals, one of them being me, could move forward in one sense or another. Although a single series of books was not about to accomplish such a huge task all by itself, it was sufficient to help get the work started. What I did not understand at the time was the individuals I saw, in my dream, zooming skyward were not just representative of solitary entities. They were entire communities and countries weighed down by chains of apathy and self-consuming dehumanization. Oddly, they were as desperate for liberation from the impulse to feed off the misery of mortals as the millions of black, white, brown, yellow, and red faces before them to be freed of their captors' grotesque addictions to insanity. The option to wake up and make the better choice seemed the easiest thing to do in the world and yet favor seemed far too often—and so clearly unnecessarily—to go to its opposite.

B&W digital watercolor of Dr. Abigail Jordan, founder of African-American Monument Committee and The Consortium of Doctors, by Aberjhani.

The Bridge and the Monument: a Tale of Two Legacies

"We have skeletonized because it is easier to remember history that way, and Georgians and others have erred in the interpretation of themselves because of that propensity."

—George Anderson, *(The Wild Man From Sugar Creek)*

The incongruences and idiosyncrasies of history's fondness for irony are rarely as evident as when standing next to the African-American Monument on River Street at night in Savannah, Georgia, and looking westward at the glittering beams of the Talmadge Memorial Bridge. Some 100 yards or so in the opposite direction, off to the southeast beneath the area known as Factors Walk and facing municipal administrative offices, are the circular red brick structures which local myth used to describe as holding pens in which, reportedly, Africans were often kept upon their arrival to Savannah during slavery and until they were sold as slaves. A contemporary marker placed there in recent years has identified them as the Cluskey Vaults, named after Irish architect Charles Blaney Cluskey (circa 1808-1871). Citing lack of any known evidence slaves were once housed in the vaults (as they unquestionably were in other facilities in the Historic District area), researchers determined they did indeed function primarily as storage but may also at various times served as stables, trash dumps, or even temporary camp sites for Union soldiers.

In keeping with the custom of refraining from naming public monuments after living individuals, the African-American monument was not named after Dr. Abigail Jordan (1925-2019) the black woman whose decade-long drive to provide Savannah with its first monument to honor the contributions of Blacks to the city culminated with a triumphant ceremony on July 27, 2002. Nor would the unpresumptuous and patrician Jordan have had it any other way. Though her personal financial contributions to the completion of the monument and sacrifices of time and energy would certainly make such an honor appropriate, and, one would imagine, one day inevitable.

By contrast, the Eugene Talmadge Memorial Bridge is named after a man who in 1935 declined to lend his name to a highway for fear that he might end up "on the chain gang or go wrong before I die," and thus run the insufferable risk of breaking rocks and sweating all day long on a road bearing his name (Anderson, William, *The Wild Man of Sugar Creek*, p.123). While the bridge that does bear his name is a far more poetic and majestic construction than the highway proposed in the last century, it is also something of an unlikely symbol for a man who championed segregation between human beings rather than unification, and who spent four terms as governor of Georgia (though he died shortly after his fourth election) battling to hold onto the past rather than welcoming a future made unstoppable by the Great Migration and the reforms of Franklin Delano Roosevelt's New Deal.

Perched on a four-foot-tall marble base, the richly dark bronze African-American Monument altogether stands approximately twelve feet tall. It is neither provocative nor pretentious in its quiet projection of a black family garbed in what once were called Sunday go-to-church clothes but stands with the calm assurance of dignity that became a trademark of African-American cultural identity during the Civil Rights era of the 1950s and 1960s. To the uninformed, this depiction might imply that the artist, Dorothy R. Spradley, was more intent on indulging her personal creative sensibilities than on communicating a point of any particular historical significance. But it has been noted since the first publication of this essay, in *The American Poet Who Went Home Again*, the choice was determined by monument committee members. One still, nevertheless, wonders what the impact might be if, say, the two adults looming over the boy and girl were dressed in the rags of slaves and their faces, scarred, covered with expressions of fierce determination and courage rather than featureless complacency. Their broken manacles and near-nakedness would communicate something of the past political and social struggles by older African Americans on behalf of their progeny. The more modern apparel of the children could then indicate the hard-won abundant harvest of equal opportunities for employment and education, the right to vote without fear of being murdered for doing so, and more adequate healthcare and housing.

That the visual image of the sculpture does not make as potent a statement as this quote from Maya Angelou on its base in no way lessens its beauty, import, or relevance: "We were stolen, sold and bought together from the African Continent. We got on the slave ship together. We lay back to belly in the holds of the slave ships in each others' excrement and urine together, sometimes died together, and our lifeless bodies thrown overboard together. Today, we are standing up together, with faith and even some joy."

After all, the fact that it is Savannah's first such monument need not mean it must remain the city's only African-American monument. In a city where dozens of monuments pay tribute to the days of the Confederacy, the once-thriving Native American presence, and different aspects of the city's European heritage, another half dozen monuments documenting the many contributions of African Americans would be more than appropriate in different parts of the city.

The nobility, sincerity, and necessity that inform the intent behind the creation of the African-American monument stand as clearly as those behind the renovation of the bridge linking Savannah to South Carolina. What is less clear in the minds of the 131,510 citizens (now estimated at 146,444) who inhabit Savannah, and the millions of tourists who visit the city annually, is the intent behind the bridge's official name. Many assume it is named the Savannah Bridge and look with blank astonishment upon hearing it is actually the Eugene Talmadge Memorial Bridge. An indigenous African American might smile with confused pain when learning Talmadge campaigned and won offices based on a platform which championed white supremacy and that his general policy in regard to blacks was: "I want to deal with the nigger this way; he must come to my back door, take off his hat, and say, 'Yes, sir'" (*Wild Man*, 230).

II.

William Anderson, one of Talmadge's more able biographers, characterized the former governor as something akin to a sentimental folk hero. The son of Tom Talmadge and Carrie Roberts Talmadge, Eugene Talmadge was born into middle-class comfort on September 23, 1884. Despite the advantages of an economic and social background which allowed him to graduate Phi Beta Kappa from the University of Georgia in 1901 and to obtain a law degree in 1907, Eugene Talmadge cultivated an image of himself as a poor dirt farmer and reveled in the stereotypical language and antics of that class. He was, therefore, more likely to proclaim that he was "just as mean as cat shit" rather than state simply that he was impatient or had a bad temper. Likewise, an invitation to visit the governor's mansion was issued in a manner more commensurate with a character out of Erskine Caldwell's classic *Tobacco Road* than with what one might expect from an honored statesman: "Come see me at the mansion. We'll sit on the front porch and piss over the rail on those city bastards" (*Wild Man*, 103).

Although his pose as an incorrigible rural hick at times seemed blatantly exaggerated, Talmadge's appreciation of the culture was authentic enough that he could laugh at himself when his political rivals accused him in court of copulating with his mule. He rather admired them for the one-upmanship they demonstrated with the slogan, "You wouldn't vote for no mule-screwing sonofabitch, would you?" (*Wild Man*, 31). These brilliantly flashing colors of Talmadge's character, according to Anderson, communicated different messages to different people: "Crude, ill-tempered, profane, out of control to some, he was a God-fearing, kind, and compassionate man to others" (*Wild Man*, 98). It was this persona of a recalcitrant rural delinquent that he took with him into office upon his election to agriculture commissioner in 1926,

1928, and 1930; and, which he further promulgated upon his election to governor in 1932, 1934, 1940, and 1946.

He was also a devotee of the past whose regressive leanings did not end with racial integration but sought to discredit and dismantle those reforms set forth in President Franklin D. Roosevelt's New Deal program, recognized by most others as the single most important cure for those economic, social, and political ills brought on by the world-ravishing Great Depression. At the same time that Talmadge donned red suspenders and declared himself a champion of the white working class, he was comfortable protesting the daily wage of $1.50 the New Deal would afford farm laborers. Similarly, he opposed a pension for retired workers because he feared it would corrode the southern tradition of family members caring for their elders at home. His opposition to such New Deal programs as Social Security was total enough that he voiced his rejection of it both within the pages of his newspaper, *The Statesman*, and at the 1936 Democratic Convention. And his opposition apparently extended to Roosevelt himself as he was fond (although he later would apologize for it) of ridiculing Roosevelt's handicap and pointing out that, "The only voices to reach his wheelchair were the cries of the 'gimme crowd'" (*Wild Man*, 130).

That his assessment of the New Deal program and FDR proved erroneous even before history could have its say did not make much of an impression on Talmadge. Admitting fault was not one of his stronger points and he conceded that, "I'll never admit I'm wrong, even if I am, and I'll never apologize. If I've made a mistake, I'll ignore it and in time it'll work itself out" (*Wild Man*, 101).

One mistake he tried to ignore but which refused to simply work itself out was his decision to orchestrate the dismissal of educators Walter D. Cocking from the University of Georgia and Marvin S. Pittman from the Georgia Teachers College in Statesboro based on rumors that they were pro-integration. Despite Talmadge's declaration that he was, "not goint to put up with social equality [because] we don't need no niggers and white people taught together," (197) the Southern Accrediting System expressed its disapproval of Talmadge's attempts to manipulate the policies of higher education by revoking the accreditation for ten schools in Georgia's educational system. The conflict between the governor and the educational community cost Talmadge his bid for reelection in 1942 and during the 1946 campaign prompted students attending a speech by him to hang him in effigy. In a true indicator, however, of the political and racial schizophrenia of the times, Talmadge intensified his commitment to segregation for the 1946 campaign and on the basis of it won his fourth, albeit short-lived, gubernatorial election.

Talmadge's attitudes toward race and power can be described in many ways. A favorite contemporary euphemism for white supremacy is "traditional southern values," a term particularly effective for southern white politicians in battle for offices against black opponents, and "traditional southern values" occupied in Talmadge's heart as secure a place as anything else he dared to love. His willingness to jeopardize the state educational system, however, in order to exercise the traditional southern value of segregation, illustrated a predilection for repression and intolerance many felt bordered on fascism.

His admiration for Adolph Hitler was not a secret and his reading of the charismatic dictator's *Mien Kampf* more than half a dozen times would have won him a place of some honor among present-day National Front rightwing extremists. As if to further legitimize ideological kinship between him and Hitler, Talmadge described himself as a "minor dictator." The *Atlanta Journal* in 1942 termed his specific brand of dogmatism as "Talmadgism" and defined it as "bullying, brow-beating, dictatorship. Its reliance is not on reason but on arbitrary force..." The "arbitrary force" named here was likely an allusion to the use of the state militia to end a strike by cotton mill laborers and, in so doing, also ending their attempt to establish a much-needed union.

Talmadgism relied also, the *Atlanta Journal* might have added, on the proven sleight of hand of manipulating white people's xenophobic nightmares in regard to Blacks in order to maintain a guaranteed percentage of the white vote. The more rural and destitute the white population Talmadge addressed while campaigning or executing the duties of his office, the more frequent and brutal became his use of racial slurs. As his political rival, and another former governor, Richard Russell put it, whenever Talmadge's economic or administrative policies caused him to lose popularity before the white public, the one rallying cry always certain to garner some measure of support was, "nigger, nigger, nigger." And whether dressed in hoods and sheets or overalls stained with sweat from their labors in the fields, his constituency would gather around him like youth with cleanly-shaven heads circling round a Nazi flag.

How much of Talmadge's aggressive racism can be attributed to or excused by "the times" is debatable. Ensconced as he was in the state of Georgia's highest office and made privy to events and individuals of national and international import, it is difficult to believe he was unaware of such African-American men and women as W. E. B. Du Bois and Mary Church Terrell, or that he thought their influence upon the country a negligible one relevant only to the black race. It hardly seems possible that the virtual legion of black doctors, lawyers, educators, scientists, diplomats, journalists, and military officers making their way through such facilities as Howard University in Washington, D. C, Fisk University in Nashville, Tennessee, and Georgia's own Atlanta University system, did not serve to indicate to Talmadge not all blacks were the child-like simpletons or near-savages he claimed to believe they were. Yet the deaths of Blacks lynched year after year in Georgia during the two decades Talmadge was active in state politics remained the kind of atrocity he excused as "regrettable."

Accepting that Talmadge was a product, representative, and extension of his times increases one's comprehension of him as a demagogue empowered by racism but it does not encourage or excuse a tolerance of the bigotry, xenophobia, and repression for which he stood. A major public thoroughfare bearing his name, however, certainly makes it appear as if the city of Savannah does encourage such bigotry, xenophobia, and repression.

The Talmadge Bridge was subject to some four years of planning and design starting in July, 1983. That was followed by another four years of reconstruction before undergoing its Cinderella-like metamorphosis from a modestly adequate cantilever truss bridge to the superior performing cable-stayed highway bridge it is now, as anchored in reinforced concrete as it is in the modern technology that made its span of 1,100 feet and its length of 2,037 miraculously possible. More than a symbol of the kind of leap toward the future Talmadge distrusted so faithfully, it is a manifestation of it. Adorning such a triumph of visionary science with his name seems nearly an insult to a man who rejected modern medical equipment for rural areas because, according to him, the inhabitants of such areas did not believe in the existence of germs. As if not believing in a bullet would necessarily prevent the same from splattering one's brains if it were shot into one's skull.

III.

Interestingly enough, Abigail Hester Williams Jordan was born in an area which served as a political stronghold for Talmadge—Wilcox County, in what once was known as Middle Georgia. At the time of her birth on March 5, 1925, Talmadge was already building the political and racial momentum that would win him election as the area's agricultural commissioner the next year.

Unlike Talmadge, Jordan was not born into the material comforts enjoyed by the elite of the time, and the title of her as yet unpublished fictionalized biography, *Memoirs of A Slave's Granddaughter*, reflect that fact. She nevertheless did benefit from the labors of her self-employed father, Sam Williams, who used to make the wooden ties upon which railroad tracks were laid. She also received from her mother,

Leah Williams, who worked at home to raise her six offspring, a great deal by way of self-determination and a lack of patience with racism.

The same kind of disregard for the rights and lives of African Americans that Talmadge excused as "regrettable" eventually led to most of Jordan's family relocating to Savannah while a few remained behind to work with her father.

Her memories are clear enough of going with her mother to the Wilcox County Courthouse and watching her attempt to vote. Leah Williams was not surprised when she didn't get to vote but mother and daughter were both traumatized when a white man tripped her on the courthouse steps and caused her to fall, suffering an injury from which she never fully recovered. A visit from the Ku Klux Klan, which left its trademark calling card in the form of a cross burning in their yard, forced Sam and Leah Williams to do what so many black families have done since the days of slavery: divide in order to survive.

Jordan, however, did much more than survive. She thrived by gaining entry into a private school in Albany and washed dishes to help pay for her education there. She later received an undergraduate degree in 1949 at Albany State College (now University) and a Master of Arts degree from Atlanta University. She drove back and forth between Athens and Savannah to study for her Doctorate of Education, which she received from the University of Georgia in 1980. In the course of obtaining her education, she married John Wesley Jordan and had one son.

In 1991, Jordan was strolling down River Street when it struck her that out of Savannah's then 43 monuments, not one acknowledged the contributions of African Americans to the city's history. The closest thing to such an acknowledgement was the cobblestone street over which she and others were walking. "History has it that these stones were laid by the hands of slaves who selected and adjusted the odd shaped rocks that would accommodate the pounding of human and animal feet," she later stated. "In many instances, blood and flesh from the hands and fingers of the slaves were left in the mortar that still holds the stony material together today."

Her meditations upon this revelation, and an inability to point out, for visitors to Savannah, a monument denoting the African-American presence, created in Jordan a determination which became the central driving force of her life. In the same year she began her crusade to place on River Street a monument dedicated to Savannah's African-American legacy, Jordan also founded the Consortium of Doctors, a group of women doctorates dedicated to helping remove barriers to education and employment among black youth. At its first induction ceremony on Saturday, July 27, 1991, the Consortium welcomed approximately fifty-four members. Eleven years later to the date, also on a Saturday, July 27, 2002, Jordan's dream to see the monument unveiled on River Street became a reality. Media representatives from around the world either attended the event in person or scheduled phone interviews with the founder to report the historic event.

Three years following the monument's unveiling, city officials, state representatives, and out-of-state dignitaries gathered again at the site of the monument on River Street and loudly cheered as a black mayor, Otis S. Johnson, declared July 30, 2005, Dr. Abigail Jordan Day. That the monument was not christened with her name did not matter to her. What did matter was it was there, standing as bronze and eternal as any other monument in the city for the whole world to see.

IV.

Debating the politics of naming things in Savannah, Georgia, was a favorite passion of the late historian and civil rights advocate W.W. Law. He believed that a balanced representation of the names of historically significant African Americans should be assigned to public buildings and thoroughfares and he fought to achieve just such a balance.

Upon the completed construction of what is now known as the

East Broad Street School, Law argued the school should be named after Robert Abbott, the famed black publisher of the *Chicago Defender*. He considered the possibility that when black, white, Asian, and Hispanic children inquired about the name of their school, they would learn how this black man born on St. Simon's Island and raised in Savannah made his way to Chicago, then, with only twenty-five cents, started a newspaper which grew into one of the most influential in the world. They would learn how his editorials were so powerfully persuasive that he helped launch and maintain the Great Migration of African Americans into the North and Midwest from the 1910s to the 1940s, a demographic shift that had no small impact on the cultural and political history of the United States. By speaking that single name and cultivating an awareness of that single individual, students might have been inspired by his examples of courage, fortitude, industriousness, eloquence, and leadership. Instead, they utter a name with echoes of other very different implications. The "street life" that has claimed millions of youth comes to mind. The determination to obscure the brave realities of black history comes to mind. And so does the danger of doing so.

Correcting the racial errors of the twentieth century—even while new ones are committed—has rapidly become one of the chief occupations of the early years of the twenty-first century (please see appendices A and B). The hue and cry of outrage that echoed from coast to coast following Congressman Trent Lott's unwitting pledge of allegiance to the country's overtly racist past reverberated powerfully enough to dislodge him from the Republican Senatorial leadership he vowed to maintain. A similar groundswell of indignation threatened to engulf Georgia's capital as the state replaced one flag sporting its sympathetic homage to a would-be confederacy with another. Although the replacement flag also honored the state's first flag of the confederacy, it somehow proved less offensive. While the state's voters presumably have no desire in these modern times to be slaves or own any, they voted to keep the new flag.

Clearly, Abigail Jordan's decade-long battle, begun in one century and concluded in the next, to provide Savannah with what truly should be the first of at least half a dozen monuments dedicated to the city's African-American heritage, is also among the corrections of errors left over from the past. Can the same be said of retaining the name Eugene Talmadge Memorial Bridge for a major public structure in a major southern city with a [one-time] population of some 80,353 African Americans, comprising sixty-two percent of the total population, and however many progressive-minded Whites?

To what degree does the name honor Georgia's historical legacies and to what degree does is simply extend one of the worse elements––racism––of those legacies? That Eugene Talmadge served his constituency of impoverished whites and fellow segregationists is not a point that can be debated. He often did so quite ably by making their voice his own and ensuring that it was heard both in Georgia and in Washington, D. C. The problem was Georgia, like the rest of the country, had never been all white, but those empowered to decide such things as the names of schools and boulevards and bridges insisted on indulging their pigmentation as though it were.

Insofar as the case in point is concerned, the name was simply carried over from that of the original bridge, which had been so christened by the Georgia State Transportation Board. Neither ignorance of the pain such indulgence causes people of color nor apathy towards it can safeguard against the violence of social catechism that generally follows when a given segment of a given population realizes it has been duped (please see appendices A and B). A sleeping giant poses little danger lolling back and forth between the comforts of dreams. Once awake and aware that it has been, as it were, bleeding for a long time from wounds to its very real and vital soul, it then poses the greatest danger of all.

It doesn't take long, once one truly considers it, to realize the bridge which shines above the Savannah River and sits like a giant tiara upon its brow is a far from suitable structure to memorialize the racism, bigotry, and regression championed by Talmadge. On the other hand, various sites where kidnapped Africans resigned themselves to life and death in slavery hell, would seem fitting indeed. Or is this observation less relevant than some may think?

In March 2006, like many cities across the United States, Savannah held "A Celebration of the Civil Rights Struggle: 50 Years Plus." The theme of the celebration was "Then, Now, Transition, Future." To commemorate this event paying such noble tribute to the legions that fought for civil rights equality, its organization committee published a handsome 56-page journal that contained a listing of programs, timelines of the civil rights struggle, and recognitions of African-American firsts in Savannah. The image on its cover was of the African-American Monument, symbolizing the strength and courage of a people's past rather than their degradation, and promising a future of shared love and humanity rather than one of divisive bigotry and oppression.

Cartoon from 1949 *Riders' Reader* published by former Savannah Transit Company.

Riding the Bus with Man-Boy and Shaniquananda: And Then Not

"It has become appallingly obvious that our technology has exceeded our humanity..."

— Albert Einstein

Riding a city bus can be like traveling in a communal living room on wheels. A lot of what you might experience in your private dwelling is put on public display, whether or not one wishes to view, hear, feel, or smell it. That contention is likely a lot more true in 2019 than it was in August, 1949, when what was then known as the Savannah Transit Company, later to become Chatham Area Transit (popularly known as CAT) published in its *Riders' Reader* newsletter a cartoon showing a dozen passengers on a crowded bus. Eight women and men with scowling faces, holding groceries and brief cases, are pressed against each other as one man casually leans with his back against them while reading a newspaper.

The large-font caption states: "Please move to Rear!" Everyone in the cartoon appears to be white; there is no apparent reason to believe the caption has anything to do with the former Jim Crow apartheid policy of forcing African Americans to move to the back of a bus in deference to the privilege granted white Americans. That there appear to be no black faces in the image at all does speak to the long-time practice of minimizing public representations of Blacks' historical majority presence in the city, one of the principle drivers behind Dr. Abigail Jordan's decade-long campaign to establish the African-American Family Monument on River Street.

The one man in the cartoon preventing everyone else from being able to move to the rear, and thus from being able to enjoy a comfortable ride, smiles while reading his paper. He is completely oblivious to the pain he is causing, or the rage he is inciting. The situation is not so different from the intimate complications of what sometimes unfolds behind closed doors. This cartoon, however, may serve as one emblem not only of a by-gone era, but as evidence of how history and change remold circumstances to create new stories and possibilities.

The Experiment

In 2011, sixty-two years after the publication of the cartoon, I set out to conduct an informal research and observation experiment designed to identify communication styles and habits of people riding public transport buses in the city. Another component of the experiment was to test my theory that developing technology was lending more substance to the assertion that public transportation could be like sitting in a communal living room on wheels. Actual families shared and concealed a lot in such a setting and people had been known to do the same in the back seats of taxi cabs. By the time of this experiment's launch, CAT had gained a reputation as one of the best public transport systems in America. Only one year before, it had added eleven state-of-the-art Gillig hybrid buses to its already impressive array of transport options, which by then included a shuttle system for getting around the downtown area and the Belles Ferry system for going back and forth across the Savannah River from world-famous River Street to Hutchinson Island. It was a definitive measure of a certain kind of progress. But what about other kinds measured more by evolving or stagnant customs and behaviors?

This subject interested me because I had noticed how odd the dynamics of interaction between us were evolving as the use of cell phones grew more popular in American culture. It was not, for example, unusual to see strolling through parks couples who were physically together while engaged in passionate telephone conversations with someone elsewhere, then end the call and for the most part completely ignore the person beside her or him. People had also started to discuss in front of strangers some of the most intimate details of their lives whether standing in line in a store, sitting in doctors' offices: or on a bus. The use of cell phones seemed to have led many to rearrange their sense of privacy and boundaries in what struck me as some very odd—albeit at times comical—ways.

At a totally opposite end of my operational theoretical and geographical spectrum, participants in the 2011 Arab Spring had used communication technology as a primary means for effectively organizing protests. What, then, while conducting a bus-riding experiment in Savannah might be the chances of discovering citizens were having heated debates over the recent execution of indigenous native Troy Anthony Davis, expressing concern over the shrinking numbers of Blacks in the city, strategizing ways to change the name of a certain bridge, or working on plans to reduce poverty in the region?

To observe, for my experiment, the greatest cross-section of people possible, I conducted it the first week of a month in late spring. The first week of any given month is when many people still venture out on buses to deal with such domestic issues as paying rent or utility bills, shopping for groceries, or running other life-sustaining errands. This adds to the traffic flow of those who ride busses on a more regular basis as a primary means of traveling back and forth from jobs, schools, or doctors' appointments. To further increase the likelihood of checking out a good-cross section of the city's Black, White, Latino, Asian, Native American, and Indian/Hindu populations, I positioned myself at a bus stop downtown on east Broughton and Abercorn Streets in front of what I recalled had been the old Woolworth store.

As a child, I had gone to the store with older siblings to get the kind of gifts many poor black kids bought for their parents on Mother's Day and Father's Day: small plaster figurines, ceramic plaques with the Christian Lord's prayer on it, plastic flowers, handkerchiefs, and other cheap but pretty and endurable pieces of bric-brac which eased the pangs of impoverishment with the balm of standardized beauty.

Now, the store appeared to have been divided in half with a shoe and clothing outlet on one side, and a popular chain sandwich shop on the other.

On that spring day in 2011, while writing discreetly in a wire-bound notebook with a leather bag hanging off my shoulder, I jotted down that out of a dozen people either standing or walking nearest to me at a given moment, eight or nine were black. The observation at the time was made more in contrast to the much smaller number I would have seen as a child when, rather than clash head-on with the ruling dictates of Jim Crow, African Americans in the city were more likely to shop at places like the Jewish-owned variety store Yachum and Yachum on what was then West Broad Street and is now Martin Luther King Jr. Boulevard.

Unknown to me as I stood penning notes was that within the next three years, the orange-painted bus stop on which I leaned would be gone. Moreover, instead of seeing eight or nine black people within touching distance, one would have to walk an entire block on Broughton Street just to count four, five, or possibly six. Half of these would be people on the clock: delivery-men or delivery-women investing in their existence if not, as most like to put it, earning a living. For now, however, the bus stop was still here and a woman with a cell phone to her ear walked up to me and asked, "You seen that 14 Abercorn bus go by yet?"

"No I haven't but I just got here, so I don't know if it's gone or not."

Her attention went back to whomever was on the other end of the call:

"He said he ain't seen it. Wait a minute, let me look down the street, this might be it comin' now, hold on. I can't tell yet. I'ma stay here and wait cause Meeka said she was gettin' on the 14 and gon' meet me right here after I got off work so we can go in this store and get whatever those tennis shoes is. Unh-huhn. I told her if she made a B or A on that test last week she could buy these tennis shoes—right?—but if they look too much like boy shoes I ain't buyin' em no matter how much she ball her face up. I don't know why she like to wear boy stuff so much..."

The bus she had spotted more than a block away in the middle of SUVs, sports cars, horse-drawn carriages, bicycle-powered carts, strolling tourists, and local pedestrians was not the 14 Abercorn. Another behind it was and, sure enough, there was a fifteen- or sixteen-year-old Meeka ready to get outfitted with new kicks in exchange for a more respectable GPA. Similar scenes of people, most often black, using the bus stops at specific locations as rendezvous points to meet friends or family members could be seen up and down the street. So could a number of panhandlers and seemingly homeless people who looked like they were amused by the discomfort their "have-not" status caused those who appeared to be in the "have" category.

One of the less popular but most accessible rendezvous points might have been toward the west end at the corner of MLK and Broughton where the Chatham County Courthouse Annex was located. Here, associates or friends, very often black men, who had not seen each other "for a minute" reconnected over stories about the number of children for which they were now paying child support. Depending on an individual's disposition, they might laugh or curse when declaring one or two benefitting from their hard-earned funds were not their offspring.

"That's alright though, somebody gotta take care of our babies man."

"I know that's right. Bitches always be talkin' 'bout how niggaz ain' shit but you don't hear 'bout the ones like you an' me who step up when we—"

"When we ain't even the ones supposed to be steppin' up. Ain't that some shit!"

"You know it is dawg! You know it is!"

"But I can use me some part-time dollars man, you know anybody hiring?"

The bus I had opted to ride for the experiment was the 24 Thunderbolt, which had stops at several senior citizen assistance homes, like the Veranda Apartments just off Bee Road and Henry Streets, and major grocery stores before heading out to Savannah State University and journeying to Whitemarsh Island Towne Center before turning back around. From where I boarded, it would stop just around the corner at the Urban Health Center before heading through the adjoining neighborhoods.

Man-Boy

Some fourteen passengers were already en route to their destinations when I got on the bus, put my dollar in the meter, and sat down halfway toward the back, almost adjacent to the middle exit door. As good as the chances were nobody actually cared what I was writing, I instinctively pulled from my bag the copy of Brian Hine's *God's Whisper, Creation's Thunder* I had been carrying around for reading company at the time and placed it on top of the notebook. I counted a seating capacity of twenty-eight but just like in the *Riders' Reader* cartoon the bus could accommodate another dozen or so standing up. Half a dozen cameras added to the sense that I had stepped onto a the set of a family reality show on wheels. The vast majority of passengers were black with no more than two whites. One man appeared to be Latino, or possibly Hindu Indian, or maybe a combination thereof. The first words I heard from anyone else came from a young man answering his cell phone at the back of the bus:

"Hello? Hey man what up? No, no, I can't do that today yo."

His voice reminded me of one of my nephew's and I turned slightly to make sure I had not failed to recognize him, or him me. Seated at the very end where the engine rumbled and snorted was a young man who looked to be in his early twenties, light copper skin, a body toned by regular work out with weights, and lines of braids neatly-styled toward the back of his neck.

"Remember what I told you?" he asked whoever he was talking to. "I gotta go see this probation fool and explain why I don't need no job. I done worked before, slavin' ain' no thang. Huhn? No niggah you know my situation, all three my women say they don't want me gettin' no job 'cause then I be gone too long."

Say what? *Gone too long*?

"Oh yeah? Who told you dat? Man muthafuckaz be talkin' too much. That's a lie, I didn't hit her! I wanted to cause I was mad as hell when I found out what she done did but before I could go off on her, right, she started workin' that lollipop and I couldn't stay mad man. Shit!"

How many of these passengers could hear this while wishing they could not? How many listening were envious over the possibility that what he was saying was true: he did not work because several women insisted on supporting him in exchange for his romantic attention? How many wanted to hear, or wished they could see, more? And lastly, how many pitied him because they knew eventually his line of reasoning was not going to fly with the probation officer and, unless he stopped depending on his muscles and penis to feed and clothe himself, at some point he likely would end up back in jail?

For the sake of my experiment, I wrote down his words without judgment and thought of August Wilson sitting sometimes in bars where he would mentally record patrons' conversations and later transcribe versions of them into dialogue for plays. If I were to put this young man's exact words into a play—honestly, despite the physique he was still much more boy than man, I thought, a Man-Boy—describing how he nearly passed out during a blindingly intense erotic moment, the only place it could get staged would be an underground sex club. Yet here in this most public of venues, any number of passengers were getting a free verbal preview almost as explicit as a clip from an X-rated movie. It was not the kind of conversation that would take place in most family living rooms and it certainly would not have made those characters in the 1949 *Riders' Reader* cartoon inclined to vote for desegregation had they heard anything even slightly resembling it.

Even so, I was at the same time reminded of Louie the Madman, a bus-riding character I had written about for a short story in my first book, *I Made My Boy Out of Poetry*, and again in a poem for *Visions of a Skylark Dressed in Black*. Now, I started to wonder if the population of Louies was increasing in the city just as various studies were beginning to indicate policemen around the country were responding more frequently to situations where mental health experts were needed rather than law enforcement officials.

"Man I shouldn't even be talkin' bout that right now cause I'm on this bus gettin' hard. Holla at chu later."

Although Man-Boy had spoken loud enough for others like me to hear him in the middle of the bus, I understood he had also spoken to some degree in code so that the details of his personal affair had remained, to his mind perhaps, semi-private. A few minutes later, another black man sitting across from me pulled out his phone—which I had not heard ring— looked at the caller ID, then answered in a muffled voice, "Hello?"

He wore a stylish business suit that indicated riding the bus might be unusual for him. The elegant watch on his wrist and single ring on each hand implied that somewhere to go along with these was an expensive car. He looked around and seemed embarrassed that he was talking on a phone in public. When he looked at me, I glanced quickly away. Though he lowered his voice, I still heard him say, "Tell Tom the file is already printed and in an envelope right there in his in-basket. I'll call you back in thirty minutes." He looked like the type who would pull out a magazine or newspaper to bury his face in while riding public transportation, like one of the seated figures in the cartoon, except he chose to lean to his right while staring introspectively out the window.

Clearly, his had been a work-related call he only answered out of concern something important required his attention. A few minutes later, the bus stopped not far from the Urban Health Clinic and five elderly black women lined up to board it. I had seen them on the bus before; they apparently lived in the relatively new Veranda apartment complex constructed in the space once occupied by the old Stubbs Tower demolished in 2007. Designed to accommodate economically-challenged senior citizens, it stood about a block from the Truman Parkway. One passenger moved down from the front seats reserved for the elderly and the physically challenged so the women could all sit near each other. The last of their group paused before sitting down and called out, "Good afternoon!" to everyone as though she were entering a neighbor's or relative's house, or about to address a church congregation. Nearly everyone, in classic call-and-response style, answered with the same words.

Shaniquananda

Just around the corner from the health center, on Oglethorpe Avenue, the bus stopped again and two young women boarded. The first, dressed in a white top and sky-blue shorts with cuffs just above her knee caps, brightly-colored bracelets that jangled on one wrist and leather, beaded, and stringed bracelets on the other, sat directly behind me and placed the buds of an iPod into her ears. Her long bound braids were pulled to one side and trailed down her right shoulder. The second was dressed in cut-off jeans with dangling threads and a white t-shirt tucked into the waistband. The clothes made a strange contrast with the elegant dark auburn braids arranged to resemble a large flower on the left side of her head and loose shiny curls tied together with multi-colored shoelaces on the other. Grinning, she held a cell phone to her ear as she put money in the fare meter and looked back toward the first young woman with a wide-eyed expression that said, *Girl you not gonna believe this!*

She and the other young woman, with their deep brown complexions and eyes like chocolate diamonds, on the surface looked enough alike to be sisters or cousins somewhere between nineteen and twenty-three years old. Their style of dress, body language (the first quietly restrained, the second happily provocative) would have made anyone paying attention think differently. If the Man-Boy at the back of the bus had talked himself into a state of sexual anxiety earlier, I imagined the voluptuous curves bouncing up the aisle might be making him even more uncomfortable. For whatever reason, the first young woman stood up to let the second sit closer to the window, directly behind me.

The way things were turning out made me think it might have been better if instead of Hine's book, I had brought along *Delicious Laughter*, one of the early volumes of Coleman Barks interpretations of poems by Rumi. A strong sense of humor, something told me, could be useful right about now. Then the young woman, as if on cue, blurted out loud enough for everyone within a few seats to hear, "Who told you that lie?!"

Hmmm, another lie, just like whoever had outed Man-Boy. Her tone of voice was both giddily outraged and confrontational, which made me uneasy sitting in front of her because the idea of discretion or boundaries obviously held no meaning for her at all. The question was, how far was she going to take this drama?

The businessman across the aisle rang the bell. As he got up to leave, his eyes rolled toward the young woman on the phone behind me when she said, "Now see, there you go trippin' again getting' all heavy and shit when we ain't even got it like that! What's wrong with you boy? You hear this shit LaGina?"

The businessman exited the bus and LaGina said in a fierce subdued tone, "Shaniquananda, stop talkin' so loud! Who dat is anyway? Tell him you'll call him back."

Within LaGina's voice was a lot of the discomfort any number of people might have been feeling at that point but which no one else wanted to address.

"Girl this Ricky! I don't know why he be trippin' trying to lock me down. Why you trippin' so hard Ricardo? Is my pussy so good you don't want me givin' it to nobody else?"

"Shaniquananda! Get off the phone."

"LaGina shut up, I'm tryin' to hear this crazy bitch."

Having grown up listening to Richard Pryor's over-the-top bawdy comedy, it would have been hypocritical of me to be shocked by her words. The woman driver appeared too preoccupied navigating through the midday traffic to have heard or cared. What left me stunned and sent my mind scrambling to assume social-scientist mode was how comfortable Shaniquananda had been speaking as she had in the present communal setting. I immediately compared her total disregard for my own gray-bearded presence and that of the elderly women, only a few feet away near the front, to someone of my generation at her age. A person of my generation at the same age would have fainted before those words could have come out of her mouth in front of people clearly old enough to be a grandparent or great-grandparent.

The seats of the elderly women were lined vertically along the side of the bus so they faced each other and could, at the same time, easily look down the length of the bus if they wished. Several of them winced upon hearing how exceptional Shaniquananda's genitalia was supposed to be but they kept their gazes trained steadily in the direction of the driver as though their souls' salvation depended on it.

Their years seemed to place them a couple of decades ahead of my own. When they were growing up during the 1940s and 1950s, it would have been customary for such an elder to scold a younger person for language considered vulgar or even to slap her face and tell her she should be ashamed of herself. Indeed, somewhere at that very moment in the city in a living room that was not on wheels, someone was likely doing exactly that to a preteen or adolescent who had no idea why the elder was getting so upset over hearing them gleefully chant words broadcast on the radio all day long.

Studying the faces of the women, what disturbed me more than anything else was the feeling they were not just embarrassed by what they had heard. They were terrified of the person who had said it, and their terror crumbled the shield of my objectivity so that I wanted to do what they once would have. The transgression was less about "respect for one's elders," which no longer seemed the social given among youth in southern African-American communities it had once been. It was, at that moment, more about the fact that any number of the elderly ebony souls in this group, possibly all them, had marched in the heat and cold, tripped over each other to avoid snarling police dogs, withstood the blasts of water cannons, cried and prayed together to renew faltering strength, and suffered repeated indignations and humiliations to secure the legal right for them sitting up front, Shaniquananda behind me, and the three-woman Man-Boy stud toward the back, to occupy their chosen seats without fear of becoming victims of hate.

Of what were they now victims? Ignorance? Political naivety? The inevitability of historical change that did not restrict itself to racial agendas or cultural preferences? On this day it was hard to tell. A subcultural mindset had evolved out of conditions and manipulations beyond any of their control: the 1980s and 1990s drug wars, for example. These had first targeted black communities as dumping grounds for illicit substances, after which black men who followed the initial lead of non-Blacks were classified as drug-war criminals. They were then promptly locked away with sentences far surpassing those of white ringleaders and various drug-manufacturing counterparts.

The soldierly old women before me could point to the long-time practice of economically disempowering Blacks and making it all but impossible for them, especially the men who were less likely to receive the supplemental assistance afforded the women who had their children, to sustain families or even single-occupancy households. There were, moreover, the enduring public symbols and indicators, such as the enshrinement of Eugene Talmadge's brand of white supremacy by placing his name upon a bridge as if to make sure the practice of racial bigotry crossed over safely from one century to the next. This last appeared to imply that, in the minds of many power-brokers, Black Lives would never matter, and therefore how African-American youth behaved toward African-American elders was inconsequential. In truth, some took it to mean how they abused or discarded their own lives did not matter.

The grief on the faces of the matriarchs was so painful to witness that I had to resist abandoning the notes I was writing to draft a poem instead. Adapting, or failing to adapt, to the volatile social climates and strategic political assaults which had hounded their supposed golden years could only have felt tragic as members of one fragment of a population within a larger dominant demographic which apparently prided itself on sustaining regression rather than fostering progression.

Undoubtedly, several of them had grandchildren or great-grandchildren, or nieces and nephews, who might be very much like Shaniquananda and LaGina, one loudly vulgar and the other striving to project dignity. They might have attempted at one point to correct the youth related to them and found themselves promptly cursed or physically threatened. They each had an extremely haunted expression of struggling to avoid looking like they represented a challenge of any kind in order to discourage any potential resulting violence. The more I stared at their faces, the more I began to argue with myself about turning around and asking Shaniquananda to please lower her voice. I also feared she might respond violently simply because she may have been raised in a living room where violent responses were typical and I was trying to decide whether I would be able to resist responding in kind.

About ten agonizing minutes later, just before reaching the Truman Parkway underpass, the issue was settled for me when two of the older women pulled the bell at the same time and the entire group all got off together to head for their senior apartment complex. Without the conflict created by an instinctive need to protect them, I relaxed and realized that since boarding the bus downtown at least as many riders had gotten on as off of it.

Shaniquananda did lower her voice some but not so much that I could not hear her laughingly ask Ricky how he thought he was going to take care of her and her two children if they got together. Unlike Man-Boy and his three lovers, she could not overlook any financial aspect of a possible relationship. On top of that, what made him think the babies' two fathers would welcome him into their domestic fold? The two of them had smoked some good weed and had fun doing it so they should just leave it at that.

As if she had been talking to me, I opened my book and skimmed pages. Many of the quotes by Rumi which Hines had employed to make his case for notable similarities between modern physics and ancient mysticism were known to me from volumes of Maulana's work I had collected over the years. What caught my attention this time was a passage from Hines' prose: *"The worlds of nature and human technology both are composed of a myriad variety of separate entities. We speak of love and living together as one family of man, but murder and mayhem stalk the streets, prejudice and pride suffuse our minds. Given such conditions, it becomes difficult to believe that everything outside of us and everything inside of us is one and the same—God." (God's Whisper, Creation's Thunder, p. 130)* One of the great enduring mysteries, I thought, that made life so unavoidably interesting.

Five minutes later I rang the bell. Getting off the bus, I went first to the post office, and then picked up a few items from the grocery store. I caught a second bus going back toward the downtown area to my residence. It was more crowded than the first because school had let out and a small crowd of students filled the back of this one. Their conversations were a little loud and rapidly-chatty but not obscene.

When one of them started to get too noisy, another said, "Oh no Miss Thang you not embarrassing nobody on this bus!" And another added, "No you ain't, you gon do a whole lot better than that!"

This seemed to work because both the reprimanded student's tone and choice of words instantly changed. I was almost as stunned by their display of protocol as I had been by Shaniquananda's and Man-Boy's uninhibited crudeness. That was a mistake on my part because once again I had allowed myself to be emotionally swayed by observations when for the sake of my blown-apart experiment I should have remained as objective as possible. But if I were to be honest with myself, objectivity had gotten crushed on the first ride when it was pinned between the rock and hard place of giddy disregard and traumatized sensibilities.

Had my experiment been an official social science inquiry and ended with one bus ride in one part of the city, a concluding report would have noted that Blacks made up no less than 95 percent of the patrons at any given time. Additional highlight would have noted the loud vulgarity of a couple and the soft-spoken eloquence of others. My earlier comparison of transportation shared among strangers to a communal living room on wheels likely would have been discarded because of the too-frequent dismissal of any sense of boundaries or mutual respect. What might have stood out then, and has come to do so since, is the role the buses played in my hometown when it came to functioning as points of connectivity, access, and interaction with demographic cross-sections.

The Unforeseen Variable

The nature of ongoing experiments, as with the nature of life, has been known to change with the introduction of unforeseen variables. One such variable was the opening of the Joe Murray Rivers Jr. Intermodal Transit Center on October 7, 2013, hailed as "the culmination of a transportation dream."

Located at 610 West Oglethorpe Avenue, the center is situated in an area filled with the historical, social, and diverse elements that define so much of Savannah's unique southern cosmopolitan character. Just a block to its east runs the boulevard named after Dr. King. In its much earlier incarnation as West Broad Street, it had been considered the hub of the city's black community with black-owned businesses that included barber shops, theatres, stores, night clubs, banks, restaurants, and a great deal more. What remains of that period exists (as of this writing at least) primarily in museums like the Ralph Mark Gilbert located at 460 MLK Boulevard and the WW Law Foundation two blocks away.

More prevalent than anything indicative of the accomplishments that once made the area comparable to New York City's neighborhood of Harlem in its black hey-day are different Savannah College of Art and Design facilities, fast-food restaurants, and tourism companies. On the opposite northeast side of the facility is the Yamacraw Village housing project, named after the indigenous Native Americans who welcomed the first Europeans to their shores. Now occupied by low-income African Americans, the project was often referred to as an incubator of violent gang activity. Just a little further in the same direction looms the Eugene Talmadge Memorial Bridge.

The new transportation center itself was named after a then living African American. The official resolution naming the facility, adopted March 9, 2012, declared that Mr. Rivers (1939-2017) , "was, and has been for at least 15 years, one of the steadfast visionaries in the forefront of advocacy for a centralized public center to serve CAT's [Chatham Area Transit Authority's] public transit system and its deserving patrons... working over the years with all the constituencies and stakeholders with an interest in the development of such a public transit center..." Despite the declaration going against the general municipal rule of refraining from naming public facilities after living individuals, it is doubtful anyone held a grudge very long against CAT officials for acknowledging Rivers' years of dedicated labor on behalf of his community. It was, in fact, a rare form of public acknowledgement of a non-celebrity African-American man's contribution to the city.

There were and still are, however, those black- and brown-skinned bus-riding constituents who later questioned whether the ultra-modern transportation center was constructed for their benefit or that of everyone except them. Should the failure to make their voices heard in any authoritative way while development of the center took place be viewed as anyone's fault other than theirs? The answer perhaps can be traced back to how well African Americans in the city, like so many in any number of America's cities, have been positioned to exercise power over their lives and destinies, or been conditioned to think of themselves as perpetually power-less.

It does not take a detailed analysis of sociological and political factors to realize some of the more ostensible implications of a single white individual, John P. Rousakis, governing the city as mayor from 1970 to 1992. Or why its first African-American mayor was not elected until 1995, just over two decades after the people of Atlanta accomplished the same. Or, yet still, why the first African-American woman, Edna B. Jackson, to occupy the position was ousted after only one term while the first two black men each served double terms. Possibly one of the cultural inclinations left over from the days of slavery is a too-easy dependence on others to act on one's behalf with the assumption they will do so exercising ethical and compassionate consciousness. Impoverished African Americans in various communities are not the only people to have made that mistake throughout history.

A review of announcements posted on CAT's website indicate the organization hosted town-hall-like meetings and open houses to discuss the changes in transportation that would impact a sizable percentage of the city's resident population and visiting tourists. However, for months after the new transportation center opened, when standing at nearly any bus stop on the east, west, or south sides of the city, you would have been hard-pressed to find among waiting patrons anyone who had attended a meeting or read a website post. People who catch the earliest and latest buses to work the longest hours and earn the least pay are rarely able to attend such meetings. When mentioning the option of weighing in online, they speak of a lack of "computer savviness" and express belief that the use of any computer anywhere means making oneself a target for manipulation by corporations, the government, and hackers.

Of course most had heard about the new facility at some point on television or via print media and knew its construction was supposed to help move the transportation system forward. Officials were promising it "reduces existing traffic congestion, while allowing for more transit related parking, tourism and other downtown business opportunities." In some ways, the intermodal transportation system as a whole is an elegant complement to James Oglethorpe's grand design for the city. In a completely different way, it reconfigured patterns of communication, social interaction, and survival techniques utilized by black stakeholders who heavily relied on the system in ways they perhaps had not consciously considered.

When standing on the corner of Broughton and Abercorn Streets two-and-a-half years before the new transportation center became operational, I had observed three quarters of the people in my surrounding vicinity were African American. After the center opened, bus stops were removed from Broughton Street ostensibly for the reasons noted and it became rare to see two or three black faces when walking the entire length of a block much less than see almost a dozen within a few feet of wherever you might happen to be standing or walking. What, then, had happened to the constituents purported served by this admiral feat of technology, transportation, and engineering?

The kind of rendezvous that once allowed people to meet after work or school and run a quick errand to stores located just a few feet away before heading home or back to work was no longer possible. Added to the grumblings of those who actually rode buses was realization that any number of bus routes had been deleted as well. Among those no longer running was the 24 Thunderbolt where Shaniquananda and Man-Boy had treated everyone within earshot to accounts of their erotic lifestyles and where a group of elderly black women had fearfully huddled to hide their disapproval and avoid receiving public ratchet tongue-lashings in return. People who relied on the system to get within walking distance of one location for whatever purpose discovered their options severely limited. After taking care of business, unless near the vicinity for a shuttle stop, they had to make their way on foot to the bus terminal half a mile away back across MLK Boulevard for transportation back home or elsewhere.

Like any major change in any local community, state, or nation—take evolved versions of American health care laws for example—this one would require fine-tuning. Key components to that refinement likely would need to come more from the engagement of indigenous African-American constituents than that of administrators professing to serve their needs. However, people who believe they are powerless rarely attempt to exercise forms of influence outside the sphere of immediate family ties. They place their trust in the advertised intelligence and kindness of strangers-lately-become-neighbors. For that decision, they sometimes become intimately familiar with and alarmingly proficient at defining a word few claim to cherish: suffering.

B&W of *That Time We Woke Up Laughing in Claude Monet's Garden* by Aberjhani.

Monet, Vann, and Gibran at the Telfair Museum of Art

"I have only looked at what the universe has shown to bear witness to it through my paintbrush... Put your hand in mine and let us help one another to see things better."

—Claude Monet

The nucleus of Savannah's Telfair Museum of Art complex, consisting of the smaller one-time mansion at 121 Barnard Street, designed by William Jay and constructed in 1819, along with the more modern Jepson Center for the Arts at 207 W. York Street, designed by Moshe Safdie and opened in 2006, sits appropriately enough just off Telfair Square (formerly St. James Square) in the city's well-preserved Historic District. These provide residents and visitors with an experience of the cultural arts not so far removed from what museum-goers might undergo at the Louvre in Paris, France. Completing the complex of the southern showcase is the Owens-Thomas House, also designed by English architect Jay and constructed from 1817-1819, which sits some seven blocks to the east at 124 Abercorn Street just off Oglethorpe Square. Like the Confederate Monument in the city's Forsyth Park, the house stands as a testimony to the uniquely antebellum style of urban slavery that once characterized the city and is not something you will likely find in a tour of European museums.

Originally known as the Telfair Academy of Arts and Sciences, the facility is a remarkable example of America's earliest attempts at flexing its cultural muscles and putting the international community on notice that it was preparing to challenge Europe's status as a centuries-long center of standard-setting classical arts. Yet it also stands as one of those peculiar paradoxes of the American South–and perhaps of different societies around world throughout history–in that the wealth used by

Alexander Telfair's family to finance its construction as a family mansion came largely from the labor and sales of slaves. The incongruence of simultaneously claiming ownership of another human being while professing superior moral and aesthetic intelligence over the same has proven the downfall of more than one civilization in history. The erasure of such a contradictory proposal, or possibly of slavery's many ongoing systemic insanities themselves, may have played a part in Mary Telfair's decision to grant the mansion to the Georgia Historical Society for use as a museum.

That Confederate General Lafayette McLaws and his staff used it for their headquarters toward the end of the American Civil War should provide some sense of how heavily its foundation rested on the backs of Blacks prior to its conversion from 1883-1885 to a public museum. Five statues of famous artists adorn the exterior of the museum. Four of them—Rubens (1884), Raphael (1885), Phidias (1885), and Rembrandt—are attributed to the Viennese sculptor Victor Oskar Tilgner. One, that of Michelangelo (1884), is attributed to Anton Paul Wagner. They may be viewed as a kind of homage to slavery as it was practiced in ancient Greece and Rome. Despite the restrictions it placed upon the lives of the enslaved, slave-holders saw no disconnect between the institution and their claims to superior intelligence or moral character. In fact, some convinced themselves it was an affirmation of such claims.

When considering how the practices of slavery, philanthropy, and rebellion could all converge behind the exquisitely-rendered doors of the Telfair, it becomes less difficult to contemplate the different implications of it simultaneously housing works by artists as diverse as France's original impressionist Claude Monet (November 14, 1840–December 5, 1926), America's Harlem Renaissance-influenced Luther E. Vann (December 2, 1937-April 6, 2016), and Lebanon's symbolist Kahlil Gibran (January 6, 1883–April 10, 1931). Each traveled very alternate biographical and historical paths to reach the space his creative vision eventually came to share with the others at the Telfair Museum.

Even so, there is a kind of unrecognized affinity between their tinted meditations on the layered realities of human existence. It is one which hints at the ever-unfolding wonders of time's relationship with space and light's eternal dance with the shadows and hues that give shapes to perception and depths to meaning.

The alluringly enigmatic paintings, drawings, and water colors of the Lebanese-born Gibran arrived first at the Telfair when Mary Haskell, the artist's former mentor and patron (referred to by some as his lover for a time) presented the Telfair Academy of Arts and Sciences with "102 drawings, watercolors, paintings and pastels" in 1950. The bold depictions of multidimensional realities painted by Vann, who was born in Savannah and raised both there and in New York City, made their Telfair debut in 2000 when the museum acquired the paintings *With These Hands* and *Habersham & 41st*. He became the first living Savannah-born African-American artist to have a solo exhibition at the Telfair Museums when images from *Elemental, The Power of Illuminated Love,* were shown from May 16 to September 14, 2008, at the Jepson Center for the Arts. That same year, his *Summer in Eden* was added to the museum's permanent collection. The impressionistic vision of Monet in a sense preceded both Vann and Gibran through interpretations of it by international artists (including Americans) housed by the Telfair at least since the early 1900s. Paintings by Monet himself, one of France's most revered sons, made their initial, though not final, appearance as the central draw for "Monet and American Impressionism" from October 16, 2015 until January 24, 2016. For that exhibit, they shared the spotlight with early American impressionists and contemporary African-American artist Mickalene Thomas.

Yet, if only during the period that Monet's paintings were on display, they also share a singular historical moment with the works of Vann and Gibran. For the basically sedate imagination, it might not seem remarkable that the works of these three unique artists found themselves in the care of such a revered institution. Those endowed with a more animated cognizance might enjoy the richness of the historical confluence at a time when so many representations of diverse cultures are prone to clashing rather than harmonizing in any appreciative manner. The idea of a conversation between the artists' various creations might provide some amusement as well as some useful discernment. What, for example, might Monet's *Waterloo Bridge* (1903), Gibran's *Jesus Son of Man* (1916), and Vann's *Summer in Eden* (2005) have to say to each other while ensconced upon a wall and awaiting the eyes of properly-entranced viewers?

Would they focus mostly on how the mysteries of light inspired their labors and at times, perhaps, saved their lives? Or might they give even more thoughtful considerations to the role that darkness played in their unique abilities to transform blank space into profound statements on overlooked aspects of existence? It could be, if such a conversation between painted subjects were possible, that they might share war stories about battles to achieve and maintain forms of balance in life which they might then transfer to canvas. Or, it could be, that they might share some usually hidden bits of insight that tell us more about their creators and ourselves than previously considered.

Anyone wishing to argue that there are no appreciative parallels between the canvases produced by this creative triumvirate could easily do so. They could point to the well-documented influence of William Blake, August Rodin, and Leonardo da Vinci on Gibran's work as well as his relatively sparse use of color. They could say Vann's intriguing dance with fragmented perspectives and unexpected juxtapositions of characters and objects was derived in part from his study of frames by Beauford Delaney and the celebrated collages of Romare Bearden. In regard to Monet, they might note his superb painted documentation of how the subtly-shifting moods of light and time revealed through his prolific series different characteristics of the same subject. They could look as well at the particular images that coaxed the individual artist to commit to canvas his most beguiling and evocative statements on the varying facets of the human condition. Such critical thinkers might even make similar statements about their biographies. Yet common to all is evidence of a journey through the thickest and heaviest of shadows to arrive at a place where each artist utters an observation in harmony with Monet's: "The real subject of every painting is light."

Gibran

The Lebanon from which Gibran's family immigrated in 1895 was more *dependent on* than it was *independent of* Syria. In the current century, Syria has been at the center of one of the bloodiest civil wars in world history and sparked a global migration that has reconfigured the population demographics of countries from Greece and Germany to the United States and Canada. In many ways, Lebanon was in 1895 like an extended territory of the larger country. With the "great massacre" of 1860 having taken the lives of more than 30,000 Christians, the motives that drove the future author of the *Prophet's* family to make its way to the legendary entry-point of Ellis Island, New York, and then to Boston, were perhaps only slightly less severe than the ravages of civil war which, between 2011 and the beginning of 2017, drove more than four million people out of Syria, including into Lebanon itself.

Accounts of the future author and artist's childhood in the village town of Bsharri are sometimes conflicting. There are those which portray him as coming from an affluent background that allowed him to enjoy exceptional privileges while others indicate that his mother, Kamila, brought him and his three siblings to America to escape impoverished conditions and a reportedly negligent alcoholic patriarch. One observation not in dispute is the uniqueness of his hometown's fabled natural environment and its surprisingly (to Westerners anyway) religiously diverse population. Before various attempts at dominance by different political and secular figures led to hostile conflicts, Christians, Jews, Muslims, Druze, and other groups coexisted in relative peace.

Gibran himself was the grandson of a Maronite Christian priest.

As an Arab who was Christian, he (and many others like him) could be described as an embodiment of qualities most Americans would consider contradictory. The word Arab more often than not was (and maybe still is) synonymous with the words Islam or Muslim(and those words are too often erroneously, automatically, associated with violent extremism). Whatever the dominant social or political conditions may have been at a given time, memories of the cedar-covered mountains for which his homeland has been famous at least since *Biblical* times and the traditions of Maronite Christianity into which he was born remained defining elements within Gibran's consciousness and art.

A childhood incident sometimes cited as one which helped define his respect for and devotion to the spiritual legacy of Jesus Christ, as well as confirm broader metaphysical convictions, was when at the age of 10 he fell from a scaffold off the side of a mountain. The injuries resulted in a prolonged recuperation that included re-breaking a shoulder bone which had mended in a crooked position, and, being placed on a wooden brace that later conjured for the artist-poet images of himself as someone who at a young age had survived being crucified: "An ordinary splint became a cross, and the painful period of convalescence stretched to 40 days—the period that Christ spent in the wilderness. The transposition eloquently illustrates the degree to which biblical legend imbued the thinking of the Maronite Christians."

Return visits to Lebanon would reinforce and amplify the sense of deep longing and mystical reverence that characterizes much of his best-known work. Unfortunately, the cultural synthesis he could celebrate as part of his being and spin into visual and literary art was not something he could do for the country or the international community as sectarian violence again shook his homeland during the late 1910s.

The needs and desires that eventually prompted Gibran's move from Boston to New York City and Paris, the places where he polished his creative talents as an artist and author, were completely different. Relocation, however, from one geographical point to another as well as from conditions of poverty and obscurity to those of relative wealth and renown, is not a guarantee of inner peace or strength. Where the creation of any accomplished artist's works are concerned, there are endeavors to balance the presence and weight of darkness with those of light. For Gibran, this is generally as true in the literal sense as it is in the metaphorical and metaphysical sense, and as prominent within his visual art as within his literary.

Light and shadow are not merely visual qualities to achieve aesthetic effects. They are spiritual and philosophical principles representative of his faith as a Maronite Christian, his exposure to the teachings of Sufism (often referred to as the more serenely contemplative mystical side of Islam), and of his individual meditations on universal truths and values which transcend secularism. He skillfully employed them to communicate, and combat, the urgent threat of extreme polarizations based on religious and cultural differences that so often, in the face of intolerance or a lack of compassion, resulted in tragic violence. He also employed them for more introspective purposes. The contrasts between light and shadow are apparent enough when viewing such solitary figures as his 1911 *Self-Portrait*, graced by benevolent presences in the background; or as in the untitled 1910 *Portrait of a Woman with Death's Head*, haunted by conditions which may be either private, or public, or both.

"In his art," observed critic Alice Raphael Eckstein, "there is no conflict whether the idea shall prevail over the emotion, or whether emotion shall sway the thought, because both are so equally established that we are not conscious of one or the other as dominant. They co-exist in harmony and the result is an expression of sheer beauty in which thought and feeling are equally blended." This harmonious coexistence between concepts and emotions are likely the result of living a life already so steeped in contrasting ideologies and types of natural beauty that within Gibran they formed innately-synthesized intuitive responses which did not require labored intellectual analysis or articulation. They had already become fundamental to his being. Speaking in 1920 with his benefactress, Mary Haskell, he offered a statement regarding critics' interpretations of his art that may have been more exaggeration than truth: "People say such complicated things about my drawings... things I never meant at all! For when I draw, if it happens that I do something a little nice or with some worth, I'm unconscious. Three or four hours after it's done I can't tell you about what it looks like. I'm not that way when I write. I do know what I'm writing, but I don't know what I'm drawing or painting." ([Hilu, Virginia (ed.) *Beloved Prophet: The love letters of Kahlil Gribran and Mary Haskell.* NY, Alfred A. Knopf, 1972, p. 321)

The sublime harmony Raphael Eckstein celebrated was likely less prevalent when it came to overcoming the hurdles to completing projects and sustaining a lifestyle conducive to repeating the process over and over again. Maintaining that balance by whatever means necessary nevertheless helped place in perspective any number of personal battles, such as: the inability to reconcile with his father, and surviving the losses of his mother Kamila, his young sister Sultana, and brother Butrus all within a year and a half. It did the same when struggling to resist the urge to move back permanently to the mountains of Lebanon rather than stay in the highly-industrialized United States where he gained ever-increasing renown among both English- and Arabic-speaking audiences.

Writing and visual art, America and the Middle East, Christianity and Sufism, poverty and wealth, the past and the present, life and death, all represented well-defined dualities—just as different, or similar, variables created the same in the lives of Monet and Vann. Shadows, rather than building bridges or proposing reconciliations, extended the conflicts which upheld barriers . They consisted of unyielding intolerance for religious differences, humanity's addiction to the drug of war, and the absence of compassion that made poverty and ignorance so prevalent in a world overflowing with an abundance of natural resources. Luminosity radiated out of acquisitions of knowledge, respect for diversity, experiences of love in its myriad forms, and the potential for ordinary human beings to develop into something close to divinity. For Gibran, the tension between these dark and illuminated polarities produced both inspired creative energy and apparent bouts of depression which contributed to the very condition said to have twisted his father's behavior—alcoholism. They also reinforced the image of himself as a Christ-like figure crucified by his desire to gift the world a transformative vision capable of empowering humanity to recognize and embody a greater version of itself.

The figures in his earlier finely-rendered interpretive drawings, such as the 1908 drawing of Charlotte Teller and his 1910 self-portrait, rarely display even a faint Mona-Lisa-like hint of a smile to indicate some flavor of joy in their lives. More typical are background spectral outlines seeming to suggest haunted pasts, unrealized dreams, or lingering wounds. The drawings themselves have at times been described as unfinished, but taken as they are they may be interpreted as raw vitality reflecting essence and form. They often resemble sculptures in the process of evolving into something more sentient or permanently representative.

The *1911 Self-Portrait* makes a useful study of the implications presented by shadows and light in Gibran's life and work because of where the first falls and where the second is reflected. The deepest shadows are on the left side of the portrait obscuring that side of the artist's face, or that part of his life haunted by the deaths of loved ones, war's destruction of an idyllic homeland, and the need to meet the demands of an overwhelming destiny. The right side shines the brightest and viewers see clearly both that side of his image and the full face of the woman in the background. If the figure in the background (as some have surmised) is his benefactress Mary Haskell, it says even more about the value the artist placed upon attributes like compassion, nurturing, love, and female intelligence as each figure shines grace upon the other.

The relationship between our ordinary socially-indoctrinated selves and the potential to become something much more is evident enough in early drawings which reference the "Greater Self" in titles, or in images which depict a much larger human-like, or perhaps god-like, figure embracing a smaller one. The 1915 graphite and watercolor titled *Uplifted Figure* presents a good illustration in which viewers see the larger entity lifting the smaller straight up by the hands. In a drawing completed the following year the smaller figure appears to be either climbing onto the larger or wrestling with it. The 1917 rendering of the pair reveal the lesser entity embracing the larger more completely. Whether these symbolize the artist's relationships with specific individual's or Gibran's personal struggle between what mystics refer to as the lower self and the higher is debatable. There is no reason they cannot symbolize both. They leave no doubt, however, that even for someone still at the beginning stages of developing his craftsmanship, his basic metaphysical beliefs were already firmly in place; a major component of his self-assigned mission was to utilize them in a world crippled by chaos and hatred.

For the artist, the ultimate expression of humanity's greater potential was realized in the person of Jesus Christ, who provided a source of positive motivation on every level of Gibran's life: in his dreams while asleep, close friendships while awake, his visual art, and his literary art. The Telfair Museum's collection (as of this writing) contains no less than half a dozen images of Christ, some identified as such and some not. Among his book titles, *Jesus The Son of Man* is second in popularity only to *The Prophet*. His literary and visual depictions of Christ have attracted some controversy because of their departure from accepted portrayals of the canonical figure. Rather than a humbly-suffering passive divine soul, Gibran's Jesus is a spiritual revolutionary who judges the church as an institution overrun with hypocrites concerned only for their worldly goods and personal political power while pretending to minister to the poor and afflicted. Nathaniel, in *Jesus the Son of Man*, boldly proclaims, "It is the mighty hunter I would preach, and the mountainous spirit unconquerable." (Gibran, K. *Collected Works*. (NY: Alfred A. Knopf/Random House, 2007, p. 287) Moreover, as spoken by John the Son of Zebedee, the Nazerene was a mortal being who served as a spiritual vehicle for:

The Christ, He who was in the ancient of days, is the flame of God that dwells in the spirit of man. He is the breath of life that visits us, and takes unto Himself a body like our bodies... the Spirit who would have us live our fuller life, came unto Jesus and was with Him. And the Spirit was the versed hand of the Lord, and Jesus was the harp. The Spirit was the psalm, and Jesus was the turn thereof. And Jesus, the Man of Nazareth, was the host and the mouthpiece of the Christ, who walked with us in the sun and who called us His friends. (Collected Works, p. 273.)

On the visual side, the poet-artist's drawings of Christ portray him in different profiles, positions, and stages of life and death, including the untitled "Head of Dead Christ" (date unknown), "Christ's head and bare arm," (1920), *Head of Christ*, and two images of Christ's head with a hand suspended before him. *Jesus Son of Man* (1928) was one of the last and used as an illustration for the book *Jesus, The Son of Man*. The raised ethereal hand appears in front of the area where the figure's chest would be had it been drawn and it may very well symbolize the instrument of anointment by divine spirit which Gibran described. The profile of the head is both firmly solid and otherworldly. The facial expression is that of a man anchored in determination to accomplish a foreboding task. Light reflects off the top of his head, brow, and cheek while thick dark hair is heavily shaded. His weapons may be the unconventional ones of a passion for higher truths and sincere love for the downtrodden denizens of humanity, but these make him no less committed a warrior than would a sword or arrows or guns in the hands of trained soldiers.

Instead of leaving certain concepts to be deciphered by the images of religion, mythology, or personal ideology consigned to paper and canvases, he pronounced them in the bold statements of masterful, now classic, literary works like: *The Madman* (1918), *The Prophet* (1923), *Sand and Foam* (1926), and *The Garden of the Prophet* (1933). In *The Prophet*, addressing an orator's request that he speak to the gathered crowd about Freedom, the departing Almustafa tells them how it cannot be claimed without embracing its various existential contradictions: "And when the shadow fades and is no more, the light that lingers becomes a shadow to another light. And thus your freedom when it loses its fetters becomes itself the fetter of a greater freedom."

Each paradox finds its anchor and genesis in acceptance of the other. Opposites reconcile by affirming their separate equally-valid expressions of a single essence. Recognizing this became one way to claim peace in an otherwise tumultuous world. Through their individually-painted realms, Vann and Monet would arrive at similar conclusions, the former in regard to the physical universe and the revelation of a multiverse, and the latter concerning nature and humanity's relationship to it.

Luther E. Vann

Vann was not a poet in the same manner as Gibran. His unique use of painted composite imagery, however, prompted the *Connect Savannah* news weekly to dub him as a visionary and "a poet who uses paint as his language" (Sickler, Linda. *Connect Savannah* Cover Story, Jan 12, 2005). Anyone who stands before the somewhat androgynous individual (most likely a young woman going by the curved contours of the body) sitting on a bicycle and dominating the foreground of Vann's *Summer in Eden* (2005, 41 x 49" acquired by the Telfair in 2008) can get a sense of what was meant by Sickler's description.

A casual viewer might take his masterful study in monochromatic harmony as an affirmation that the artist leans more toward a theory of light as a preferred definitive element rather than one of darkness. Given the stunning dominant gradations of yellow and subdued shades of gold, orange, and lime that comprise the image, their assessment would be understandable. The composition by visual appearance and via its poetically-descriptive title pronounces itself with an aggressive style of something close to barely-contained euphoria. Yet the slight downward turn of the central figure's mouth along with the calmly-serious eyes and double-halo circling the head indicate that all is either much more or much less than what it seems. So do the sternly-focused gazes of surrounding characters.

The large canvas is made up of five vertical sections with the primary figure occupying most of its center and her bicycle spanning much of the horizontal lower third of the image. Just below the pedal of the bicycle is the letter "E" painted with open lines facing downward. Presumably the letter stands for the Eden identified in the title; it may also, however, represent Vann's adopted spiritual name: Early Morning Light. In the upper left corner, a pair of green and purple hands rest upon the head of a saxophone player as if administering a spiritual healing. To the saxophone player's lower left, a boy in sportswear resembling a basketball uniform walks toward an unseen objective while a man to the right of the musician stares contemplatively in the same direction with one hand against his chin.

The figures on the right side of the canvas are even more enigmatic and yet sublimely simple: a woman sits serenely in a chair as the man in front of her moves up steps, or a foot-ladder, while looking toward her instead of straight ahead as one might expect. In the final vertical strip to the right of the woman, an individual appears to be asleep with a spectral entity reaching from above toward her. This last section begins at the back of the sitting woman's shoulder's and head; the positioning and the absence of clothing on the figures, as well as the distinct texture of the section defined by a subdued grid pattern, imply they may represent a dream floating up from the woman's subconscious. Each of the surrounding characters are connected in some meaningful benevolent way as extensions of the haloed central dominant figure. Either one at any moment could utter the words, "Beauty is always a possibility but one that doesn't count until given enough love to make it real."

The painting presents viewers with a lavish exultation of sunlit determination blanketing hidden sorrows, doing so in ways similar to Monet's triumphant celebration of the same pervasive quality spread across French landscapes and waterfronts during times of war and political scandal. That the former appreciated Monet's passion for luminosity's subtle influences is evident both from the impressionistic style of many of his paintings and from the oversized volume of the French master's work that adorned the top of Vann's refrigerator at his home in West Savannah. Aside from its position as a brilliant exception within the larger body of his paintings, *Summer in Eden* revises Monet's declaration that "The real subject of every painting is light" to proclaim "The real substance of all life is light."

Yet the greater corpus of the Savannah native's output is closer Gibran's when it comes to acknowledging the strange kinship between radiance and obscurity. This may be most evident where Gibran is concerned when viewing finely-shaded pencil drawings in which one illuminated detailed figure dominates the foreground while another less-detailed entity occupies the background. For his part, Vann began each canvas with an ebony-hued base, as if mining the shadow aspects of his own personality for inspiration, before adding the explosion of colors that give paintings like *Betting On Myself* and *Cousin Ozena* their extraordinary exuberance. This technique and the resulting canvases are in many ways commentaries on struggles to effectively juxtapose different manifestations of existence as he knew it to be: a multidimensional reality. Joy and pain, inspiration and depression, knowledge and ignorance, the private and public, and a human-made heaven beside a human-sustained hell were all forms of the radiance and density which comprise material being and higher levels of often untapped spiritual awareness.

These seemingly abstract descriptions were much more concrete in Vann's life than how they at first may sound. They began with the dichotomy of having been born in Savannah, Georgia, and then growing up both there and in New York City at a time when the former was heavily segregated and the latter was still benefitting from the cultural phenomenon known as the Harlem Renaissance. The two experiences with their existential uniquenesses and fusions could complement each other as thoroughly as they could negate each other. Elation stood in contrast against, or emerged triumphantly out of, sorrow; unlimited potentials for creativity surged against politically Jim-Crow-enforced limitations; and the finite capacities of a physical universe gave way to the enticing promises of infinite mystical and scientific realms. Rather than choosing one over the other, Vann sought to adapt to both. The geographic journeys and wanderings came to stand as a metaphor for metaphysical parallels and dynamics.

During the late 1970s, when the painter was approaching his fortieth birthday, this infusion of lived data triggered a moment of "enlightenment" following a series of psychic events. These occurrences introduced him to different ways of literally seeing himself and the world. The experience was so disconcerting that he began practicing Hatha Yoga and studying texts by Swedish psychologist Carl Jung to gain a deeper understanding of everything happening to him. Frustration sent him on a three-day drinking binge that ended with him waking up in a New York jail cell. What happened next altered his relationship with reality as he previously had known it:

"I can remember being overwhelmed by the whole of what life looked like outside of jail. Everything seemed flimsier and no longer solid like before. There was a tree across the street and as I was looking at it, the bark on the tree seemed to peel away, then another layer peeled away, and another until the whole tree looked like something made out of light."

That vision planted the seeds for what would later evolve into Vann's inner/outer technique for rendering images of physical beings dwelling among those in more refined dimensions, producing a chromatic magical realism that became as natural to his paintbrush as the literary stylings of Gabriel Garcia Marquez, or those of Toni Morrison, became to their signature prose. It grew into maturity with another insight that produced one of the archetypal characters and motifs seen in his works from the late 1970s until the 2000s, and which populate the pages of *ELEMENTAL, the Power of Illuminated Love*:

"One day I was sitting and talking with someone when the wall in front of us opened up and a figure came forward wearing a kind of helmet. The image was so strong and raw. It became the first in a series of paintings. It was also the beginning of me being able to see inwardly and outwardly at the same time."

Another individual undergoing such an experience might have started questioning his or her sanity, and possibly Vann had enough reasons to do exactly that. But even a touch of madness, he reasoned, like everything else in his life was subject to serving the sacred will of art. With the achievement of this synthesis, he set about the task of documenting in drawings, on canvas, and through sculpture his "adventures and travels as a conscious spirit." The goal was not simply to mesmerize and seduce the public with beguiling images simultaneously evoking sensuality and spirituality—though his work often did exactly that—but to illustrate the underlying unity behind such surface divisions as race, religion, politics, class, and nationality.

Instead of lamenting what W.E.B. Du Bois identified as African Americans' peculiar double-consciousness when it came to acclimating one's black skin to the demands of an environment dominated by whiteness, he found ways to exploit it for the sake of his art and whatever meaningful messages it might convey. The color purple, as it was with musical genius Prince Rogers Nelson and as it is implied in Alice Walker's celebrated novel, came to represent a divine aspect of human nature present, though not often acknowledged, within everyone.

Consequently, even though many of his later canvases were dedicated to celebrating African-American culture as exemplified in history and as lived on his beloved Millen Street in West Savannah, he saw all things as multiple expressions of a single force of energetic intelligence. The precise name one assigned to the intelligence was, in the artist's painted multiverse, less important than staking a claim to one's personal relationship with it.

The flower beds, trees, and impeccably manicured lawns that surrounded Vann's home were nowhere near as expansive as the lush groves and pond that make up Monet's Giverny Garden, but they often served a similar purpose. The purple, yellow, orange, red, and magenta of select blossoms, like African violets and tiger lilies, were transferred to his palette and canvas to produce statements on human potential in the same way that Monet interpreted images of his floating water lilies to assert nature's ability to provide humanity with a healing refuge. The Savannah native also appreciated the Frenchman's passion for painting outdoors and sometimes with Gullah artist Allen Fireall set up easels and sketch pads at different marsh areas and beachfronts in the Low Country to channel the empowering energies into their efforts.

The resilience of nature's beauty in the face of mankind's penchant for waging destructive wars, leaving giant toxic carbon footprints via spreading industrialization, and practicing predatory malevolence was like the never-fading brilliance of stars that shined persistently on, eon after eon, long past the cycles of progressions and regressions that comprise recorded history. Discovering previously-hidden dimensions of light resulted in a means for restoring the individual as well as entire communities and the fractured dreams of an era. In that, Vann was much like Gibran, painting prayers that he hoped testified to possibilities greater than the conditions from which so many constantly suffered.

On a more basic practical level, accounts of creative geniuses' heroic struggles to win recognition for their work and thereby earn a livelihood from it, or to simply master their chosen craft, often inspire people because artists frequently, by their nature and circumstances, tend to fit the description of underdogs. The challenge to live a life based on self-generated aesthetic constructions of imagery, sound, or language is rarely, if ever, met with ease. In-between focused labors and any eventual useful recognition there are what the novelist Michael Cunningham referred to as "the hours" of perilous insecurity and what poet John Keats described as negative capabilities when a person "is capable of being in uncertainties, mysteries, doubts, without any irritable reaching after fact and reason." The will to engage such struggles while hoping to extract useful meanings from them represent an important aspect of what connects the aesthetic enterprises of Vann, Gibran, and Monet.

Monet

The impressionistic style of painting and accompanying movement launched in 1873 by Claude Monet and company constituted, by its nature, a rebellion against previous ways of seeing and defining humanity's experiences of the world. Eschewing the hyper-elegance and formalized standards of realistic portraits created by masters of Europe's renaissance, Monet's labors repeatedly and consistently suggested much more was available for viewing than the average artist usually captured. Light, as he came to share its story through thousands of completed canvases, pulled back curtains of fixed focus to display different facets of a complexity barely described by the word "reality." As countless art lovers have discovered for themselves over the past nearly century and a half, this observation is demonstrated easily enough when standing directly in front of an impressionist painting and then slowly backing away from it. While moving away, what may first have appeared as individual swabs and lines of pigment slightly resembling a landscape, waterscape, or garden scene, begins to take on greater depth and structure.

Like Gibran and Vann, the elements of travel, geography, war, and the dichotomy of urban landscapes versus natural settings played significant roles in Monet's development as an artist. Born in Paris, the future iconoclast, while still a child, moved with his family to the suburb of Ingouville just outside the port of Le Havre on France's Normandy Coast, which Americans inevitably associate with World War II, June 6, 1944, D-Day. Much of his life as an adult would be spent traveling back and forth between the two, capturing the nuances of fashion and architecture in the one, and the alternating tranquility and fury represented by the other. Travel (though in some cases the word *escape* might be more accurate) across the English Channel would take him as well to London in 1870 to avoid the Franco-Prussian War, and again for varying intervals from 1899 to 1901 to reflect on the scandalous Dreyfus Affair, managing each time to produce acclaimed paintings. His journeys would carry him to places like the Netherlands and Bordighera in Italy before and after settling down at his prized Giverny estate.

Yet one of his most influential ventures was not a physical excursion at all but one of the mind wherein he sometimes drew substantial inspiration from how Japanese craftsmen evoked and honored nature. The reverence and affinity for it would come to shine through his preference for painting outdoors *in plein-air.* As a result, the creation of some of his most important image series would come close to applications of the spiritual philosophy of Taoism. This could be considered an area where he and Gibran diverged notably, as the latter asserted in *Sand and Foam,* "Art is a step from nature toward the infinite." (*Collected Works*, p. 227)

As a young adult, Monet's outlook on life was not skewered by singular dramatic worldview-shaping events the way Gibran's was after falling off a mountain in Lebanon and having the image of Christ branded upon his heart and soul, or the way Vann's was defined when he experienced his psychospiritual revelations in New York City. Monet's developed gradually in his determined conscious pursuit of art as both an occupation and a vocation. His vision, however, from the beginning was nevertheless unique as someone who at a young age employed caricatures to accentuate revealing features and characteristics of prominent individuals. Later, that same exceptionally penetrating focus allowed him to render with astounding skill visual statements on the complexities of time's and light's influences on human beings and their surrounding environments.

At one end of his spectrum of productivity, Monet's focus on individuals, such as of his wife Camille or his son Jean, framed them in precise moments at specific stages of their lives, whether in youth or when approaching death. Towards the opposite end, his various cityscapes and landscapes often yielded twelve to thirty or more canvases for series of images based on a single motif, such as those of: *The Gare St. Lazare* train station (Paris, 1877), *Wheatstacks* (Giverny, 1888-1891), *Poplars* (Giverny, 1891), *Rouen Cathedral* (Rouen, 1892-1894), *Morning on the Seine* (Giverny region, 1896-1897), *Scenes of London* (England, 1899-1904), and the *Japanese Bridge* and *Water Lilies* series at the Giverny Gardens, which the artist is believed to have started around 1895 and worked on in diverse formats virtually until his death three decades later.

The four paintings by Monet displayed at the Jepson Center in 2016 were more representative of different periods of his career than a single series or motif: *Bridge at Argenteuil on a Gray Day* (c. 1876), *Maree Montante a Pourville* (Rising Tide at Pourville, 1882), *Champ d'avoine* (Oat Field, 1890), and *Waterloo Bridge* (1903). The last was part of his London series, which would also include bold renderings of Charing Cross Bridge and Britain's Houses of Parliament. The painter's production of series involved more than just exploiting a single motif for the sake of amassing impressive quantities. In works like the *Londons*, his celebrated *Cathedrals*, and *Wheatstacks*, Monet began more in-depth explorations of light and time as instruments of nature capable of adorning physical existence with metaphysical beauty and mystery.

His *Cathedrals* prompted some to speculate that he may have quietly abandoned his well-known agnosticism toward the faith, Catholicism, in which he had been baptized. He would not, however, have needed to declare himself as formally religious to appreciate the spiritual majesty of Rouen Cathedral but it is not difficult to understand why some felt he had. To get the kind of visual effects Monet mastered working with brush and hand in the early 1890s, various artists in the digital age more readily use image manipulation software. As it was, the only tool the artist used other than his sketchpad, brushes, and paint was himself. That was enough for him to render on one canvas the Cathedral as it might appear cloaked by a thick silvery fog while in others it stands more solidly like the enduring iconic presence it was and is. In addition to earning Monet a reputation as a cutting-edge master impressionist, images like those of the *Cathedrals* and *Wheatstacks* brought him renown as an important interpreter of France's national identity. By extension, the images he brought back from his extensive travels increased his fame in the international community.

The artist often immersed himself in his subject matter, no matter where he might be geographically, in such a way that he became a living extended component of the environment, letting cold temperatures, insistent winds, or even giant storming waves threaten his chances for success. Consequently, "His paintings," as biographer Paul Tucker put it, "were lived experiences, the product of his deep personal engagement with his moment." This is more-than-evident when considering the risks undertaken to create his extraordinary renderings of *The Manneporte* stone arch, and other natural formations, located offshore in a cove near the area of Etretat, some twenty-eight Kilometers northeast Le

Havre. At least once, he noted, while engrossed in capturing the object of his visual pursuit, a huge wave knocked him into the water along with his paint, canvas, and brushes. Had a digital camera been available to capture Monet emerging from the sea with yellow and blue coloring his beard, it could have been placed beside *The Manneport* as an indication of just how intertwined his aesthetics were with the natural environment.

Whether instinctive or intentional, the contrasts of the brooding ink-dark waves of the water and the bright blue-white of the sky in *The Manneport* reveal a kind of liaison between shadow and illumination which makes possible the solid earth tones of the curved stone reflecting both. The archway itself signals the necessity of each having access to the other in order to express its greatest potential. It is almost like a physical manifestation of time which has endowed matter with shape and definition as capable of revealing unseen beauty as it is of guaranteeing eventual destruction. The resulting visual discourse is not unlike those themes painted by Vann and Gibran in which incongruence leads to cohesive affirmations of beauty and unity.

What may be most phenomenal when it comes to Monet's approach to untangling ambiguities and reassembling them as balanced principles is the way the artist reversed the dynamics of his strategy. He did this by making nature an essential extension of his palette, and of the vitality required to transform intuitive concepts into concrete results. To obtain from his surroundings what he felt he needed most, in 1893 he began working more earnestly as a co-creator with creation itself by tearing down one kind of garden on his property and reconstructing a sequence of different kinds, almost exactly as if he were executing a set of living paintings. Only instead of using pigment to create an enduring work of art, he used greenhouses, the Clos Normand flower garden, a water garden, a Japanese footbridge, and a water-lily pond. These continue in the 21st century to dazzle visitors to Giverny (like Mickalene Thomas) with exquisite seasonal displays of azaleas, tulips, daffodils, nasturtiums, roses, dahlias, and other blossoms colored by nature but curated by Monet.

This impressive feat likely would have been less spectacular if the father of impressionism had undertaken it solely for the pleasure of maintaining an exceptionally beautiful landscape. Fortunately, then, for museums and individual art collectors around the world, he did it to create a source of inspiration that would last the rest of his life, like a fountain of energizing grace from which his soul could drink, or in which it could bathe, at will. From the empowerment it provided would come world-famous beguiling studies of water lilies, the Japanese bridge, and clouds reflected in the surface of a liquid.

Anyone skeptical about Monet's conscious dedication to the practice of working in concert with nature need only read (among other communications) his 1909 letter to the biographer and art critic Gustave Geffroy. In it, he discussed his intentions regarding one of his last great works, the extraordinary extended frieze panel known as *Nympheas*. The letter includes this straightforward statement: "I have no other wish than a close fusion with nature, and I desire no other fate than (according to Goethe's precept) to have worked and lived in harmony with her laws. Beside her grandeur, her power, and her immortality, the human creature seems but a miserable atom."

Whatever his chosen subject, the presence or absence of luminosity played a powerful part in what the artist experienced through his execution of the work and what he hoped to communicate to audiences through it. The same holds true when viewing the more compelling surfaces created by Vann and Gibran. In the painted visions of the French artist, the Lebanese, and the African-American, light is an illustrated language used to communicate hard-won observations about what matters the most and the least when it comes to the ever-changing human condition. Is there any real need to resist the temptation to imagine the iridescence of one communed in some sense with that of the other while they all for the first time shared common ground at the Telfair?

The vast powers of illumination are what each would have needed and desired to bridge unsettling social, political, aesthetic, and spiritual gaps in their lives.

In many of the artists' works, captured radiance reconciled the differences between violent polarities and reestablished possibilities for new perceptions and interpretations of age-old conundrums. What followed in turn were fresh opportunities for manifesting new beginnings. That possibility certainly shines through Vann's *Summer in Eden* and rebelliously declares itself in Gibran's multiple portraits of Christ. Monet's Giverny images speak clearly to the concept but might demonstrate it even better in *The Manneporte*. They all struggled to provide for themselves that which they also hoped to gift to society. Light revealed self to self as an integral part of a greater benevolent whole.

Savannah by the Twenty-first Century Numbers

"Each city or locality has its own purpose and destiny and these will be shown by its numbers."

— Juno Jordan (from *Numerology*)

Most of us understand numbers as symbols used to describe quantities. Our wallets or purses contain so many dollars (if gainfully employed or the happy inheritor of family funds). We budget resources and take dubious delight measuring various parts of the anatomy. In short, a large part of how we understand life on a daily basis hinges on an acceptance of numbers as recognizable quantities. But for enough centuries to lend serious credence to the notion, many have believed that numbers signify more than amounts. For them –philosophers, mystics, housewives, poets— numbers represent a language describing human qualities and spiritual cycles which animate our material existence. Study of the application of these qualities and cycles is known as numerology.

The late Dr. Julia Seton in her masterful work, *Symbols of Numerology*, described the practice as: "the science, philosophy, psychology and religion of life interpreted from the symbols of names, dates, and numbers." This interpretation is done by analyzing birthdates and the numbers which correspond to alphabets in a given name. Several systems are used worldwide to determine the numerical value of a letter but one of the most common is known as the Chaldean. The following chart illustrates the numerological equivalents of alphabets in the English language:

1—A, J, S   2—B, K,T   3—C, L, U   4—D, M, V

5—E, N, W 6—F, O, X   7—G, P, Y   8—H, Q, Z   9—I, R

And while the alphabets have numerical equivalents, the numbers in turn possess qualitative definitions. In abbreviated fashion, the numbers 1 through 9, along with 11, 22, and 33, would be defined this way: 1 stands for individuality and originality; 2 means cooperation or dedicated supportiveness; 3 is joyful, personal expression; 4 is service and limitation; 5 is freedom and versatility; 6 stands for love, responsibilities, and balance; 7 is penetrating awareness; 8 means material accomplishment and leadership; and 9 is selfless humanitarianism. The numbers 11, 22, and 33 are described as master numbers and defined as follows: 11 stands for spiritual illumination; 22 means master builder; and 33 represents courage, compassion, and sacrifice.

The numbers derived from an individual's full birth name and that calculated from the birthdate are considered the four figures key to providing useful insights on character, hidden motivation, image, destiny and trend patterns. The three primary numbers associated with names are known as the heart's desire number, the personality number, and the destiny (or expression) number. The figure derived from the birthdate is called the birth path number. These numbers are determined by adding up a specific sequence, such as all the consonants in a name, then reducing the total to a single digit unless the total happens to equal one of the aforementioned master numbers: 11, 22, or 33. For example, the total value of the numbers corresponding to the letters in the name Marlene Smith equal 52. The 5 and 2, as illustrated below, are then added together (described as being reduced to a single figure) to determine a Destiny Number of 7:

M A R L E N A   S M I T H

4 1 9 3 5 5 1   1 4 9 2 8

28   +   24 = 52

5 + 2 = 7

The heart's desire number is determined by adding up all the vowels in a name and then reducing the remaining number to a single digit. If the number reduces to 11, 22, or 33, it should not be reduced any further because of their designation as master numbers and the special interpretations that go with them. The personality number is taken from the reduced sum total of the consonants in a name and the essence number from the sum of all the letters in a name.

Generally, these calculations and analyses are applied to individuals but both reason and metaphysical history hold that they are just as applicable to places. Like the one in this case study: Savannah, Georgia, USA. Where the "Hostess City" is concerned, the numbers have always been interesting in the non-metaphysical demographic sense. Consider, for example, that during the hey-days of slavery, in 1825, Blacks in the city outnumbered Whites 3,203 to 2,763. Twenty-three years later, the White population took the lead with 7,150 and Blacks with 6,313. Another interesting observation from the same period is that out of the 22 African Americans in the city's history known to have owned slaves, more than half were women.

Population figures in more recent times have swung back and forth with African Americans at one point topping 60 percent and flexing enough political muscle to propel Blacks into the mayor's office after a single white male individual, John P. Rousakis, governed the city for all of two decades, from 1970 until 1991, and Susan Weiner, a white woman, from 1992 to 1995. The late Floyd Adams became the city's first African-American mayor in 1996, followed by Otis S. Johnson in 2003, and Edna B. Jackson in 2011. The numbers that vetoed Jackson's bid for a second term were not the Blacks to Whites demographic ratio, but the ones showing a nonstop rise in serious crimes which later appeared to be leveling off after Eddie DeLoach became mayor in 2016 but then proved otherwise in 2018 and early 2019. Some citizens have blamed the chronic crime issues on "failed leadership" while others say it has more to do with the city's higher-than-national- and higher-than-state-average poverty level. Critical onlookers wager the two are not completely unconnected.

Poverty in particular has remained a persistent thorn in local leaders' collective side at least since Rousakis's twenty-one-year stint and the most severely impacted have commonly been African Americans. City leaders felt they had turned a kind of corner in December 2018 when new U.S. Census figures indicated the poverty level in the city had dropped from 26.4 percent to 21 percent. But a follow-up analysis posted at the end of January 2019 on the American Fact Finder website pushed the figure up to 24 percent. Population stats also showed Savannah had grown impressively from 131,510 residents in 2000 to 146,444 in 2017. Ratio-wise, African-Americans have regained and retained their status as the majority population 79,315 to 56,759. That, however, is only one factor out of many to contemplate when studying the area's evolving demographics.

In addition to sizable Asian, Latino, Native American, and biracial populations, it is also worth noting that the median age of residents in this certifiably historic city is only 32.3 years young. How can that fact in the coming years not influence cultural behaviors and political patterns carried over from previous generations?

Nevertheless: when considering the impact which American black culture has had on different populations around the world since the height of the Harlem Renaissance (to which Savannah contributed significantly) in the 1920s and 1930s, it may be argued that demographic numbers are at least as important to the international community as to African Americans in Savannah. Whether or not, however, they recognize themselves as the history-appointed stewards of such industry-shaping trends as hip-hop and the neo-negritude wave spawned by the Black Panther movie is quite a different matter. Claiming whatever power comes with such recognition and exercising it in ways that benefit humanity as a whole could play a very important role in what a different set of numbers imply.

Love and the Heart of a City

What specifically does a numerological analysis say about the character, past, present, and maybe future of a city which was once Georgia's largest slave-trading center, and which as yet possesses the potential to become its most dynamic commercial and cultural arts center? When the city's Heart's Desire number was first calculated in 1996, it was done using only the name Savannah. Employing that approach, it was easy to determine the Heart's Desire because the only vowels in the name Savannah are three A's, each the equivalent of the number 1, and totaling brilliantly enough the number 3. This is the significance assigned to the number 3 for that first analysis:

In the case of an individual, a heart's desire number of 3 would indicate someone who harbors secret or subconscious goals to express him- or herself through the power of words. Humor, good fortune, and a strong sense of creativity would prove motivating factors in their lives. Such elements are readily visible in the life of this city called Savannah. As the birthplace of such literary talents as James Alan McPherson and Conrad Aiken, and the adopted home of writers Rosemary Daniell, the late Ja A. Jahannes, Jessica Leigh Lebos, and many others, there's clearly no shortage of writers and speakers distilling the word.

Although some local writers may have a stronger national profile than others, the number 3 as the city's heart's desire implies it is very possible that more will grow into national prominence until the city achieves the kind of world literary renown enjoyed by such places as New York, San Francisco, London, or Paris. In the case of visual art associated with the city, this is already happening to a large degree.

The problem, in retrospect, with this Heart's Desire number analysis is that it only took into the account the name Savannah. A numeroscope for a person would include the individual's full name: first, middle (if they have one), and last. Applying this to a city means treating the state in which it is located as a last name. Therefore, Georgia would function as Savannah's last name and this means the total number of vowels and the numbers to which they reduce all change. Instead of adding up only the three A's in Savannah, you have to include the additional E (5), O (6), I (9), and another A (1) from the name Georgia. The total numerical value then becomes 24, which is further reduced to 6 by adding the 2 and 4 together.

Six as the Heat's Desire number represents significant differences from the number 3 as the Heart's Desire number but also shares similarities. For a person, a Heart's Desire number of 6 would indicate someone yearning to establish a solid home and family life where love is an acknowledged and treasured value. They would be drawn to work that allows them to serve the community, such as teaching or nursing. Creativity and artistic endeavors would play an important role in their plans to maintain a safe nurturing environment for all citizens.

How does this translate into 6 as a Heart's Desire number for Savannah-Georgia? For one, the city has a history of being concerned with blending housing and creative landscapes going back to the antebellum period when a number of the still-standing Historic District architectural rarities were first built. In the next century, during the 1950s, public housing projects like Fred Wessel and Hitch Village (now the View of Oglethorpe Apartments) were constructed to present what city administrators considered to be a more hospitable appearance to visitors entering the city crossing the bridge from South Carolina. It was also civic leaders' way of taking care of the families of veterans who had fought in World War II and the Korean War. African Americans who lived below the poverty line due to Jim Crow racism benefited as well.

The tendency to go overboard on an inappropriate extension of paternalism or maternalism when it comes to municipal authority—or when social entrepreneurialism contributes to sustaining a permanent underclass instead of helping members of it progress— can be considered a negative aspect of the number 6 as a Heart's Desire qualifier. Anyone thinking that does not sound like such a bad thing needs to examine the ratio of public assistance initiatives compared to those designed to foster independent business efforts or support individual education goals.

Character and Landscape

The personality number says more about others' perceptions of an individual's character than it does about their true demeanor or behavior. Applied to a city, this refers a single serious modern concept: image. The first analysis of Savannah's personality number, again, using the consonants in the name of the city without adding those in the name of the state, concluded that it was a 5 and offered the following:

The Coastal City's Personality Number is one of the most intriguing there is. The number 5 indicates that non-Savannahians are likely to view the city as both multi-faceted and "different," even odd or eccentric in its own way. They will note not only the varieties of Spanish, English, and Oriental architecture with African-design flourishes beside well-kept parks, but the distinction of mentalities that lean more towards perpetuating personal idiosyncrasies than interacting with the rest of the country or world. Whether said perceptions come off as negative or positive may depend on how successfully denizens balance self-interest with communal interests.

The ideas of freedom and change are also important where the number 5 is involved in understanding a city's personality. If freedom or positive change appear stunted or absent to the eyes of onlookers, the result would be a visitor picking up on so-called "bad vibes." Would such vibes be good for the city, one might ask. Not likely. Does this mean the city would be wise to invest in ways that promote a truer sense of liberty and healthy diversity? Quite possibly. (from original 1996 Savannah by the Numbers analysis)

The revised Personality Number for the city adds the consonants also included in the name Georgia: G (7), R (9), and a second G (7). These added to the consonants from the name of the city equal a total of 46 that is then reduced first to 10 by adding the 4 and the 6, and then to 1 by adding the 1 and the zero.

Pertaining to an individual, 1 as a Personality Number would indicate a person whom others view as unique in ways that may be considered good or bad, depending on how their uniqueness is utilized. To the negative extreme, 1s can come off as arrogant or weird. In a more positive direction, they are perceived as independent, original thinkers, and potential leaders. In terms of a city like Savannah, it is worth noting in regard to definitions of the number 1 Personality Number that the city was one of the original thirteen colonies. State founder James Oglethorpe at first prohibited slavery in Georgia and his enlightened approach made the colony stand out in contrast to surrounding areas where it was allowed.

Modern-day Savannah possibly fits the Personality Number of 1 more accurately than the previously-calculated number 6. The most obvious reason is because the debilitating divisions which continue due to race, class, and stunted upward mobility for so-called have-nots fail to live up to the cohesive sense of community associated with 6. The singular historical character of the city has played a major roll in the success of such enterprises as the *Midnight in the Garden of Good and Evil* bestselling book and in its currently growing film industry. From that perspective, the uniqueness associated with 1 projects a positive image generating positive results. The city's primary challenges in this context are how best to share the benefits of its distinctiveness with a residential population that is far more heterogeneous than homogeneous, and how as a leader—whether Black, White, Latino, or Asian—to address racial issues without allowing them to dominate every decision when governing for the benefit of all.

From Slavery to Where?

The third key number in Savannah's numerological profile is its destiny number. The original analysis identified this number as 8 and proposed the following breakdown:

For a person, the number 8 would denote someone with a strong potential to act as a leader, organizer, or executive with a talent for accumulating wealth. For a city, it would signify a relatively stable economy ensuring financial equilibrium for most of its inhabitants. Unless: a small group of well-to-doers made it a point to hog the majority of resources and cash flow. In such an event, the spiritual side of this metaphysical equation would become unbalanced. Excessive criminality, racism, sexism, classism, and other social ill-isms would then mar the city's communal life. This would not be corrected until a sense of spiritual, philosophical or social responsibility is employed to create the necessary equilibrium. In other words, too much greed from a single corner of society in a city, state or country would throw everything else out of whack. Does Savannah (or any city with 8 as its destiny number) have a problem in this area? Residents might want to close their eyes and meditate on the question.

Interestingly enough, although the Destiny Number changes with addition of the letters from the name Georgia, it is the same for what is called the Approach Number. This figure describes the strategic or instinctive approach a person, or a place, employs to achieve a goal, tackle a problem, or conduct regular daily affairs. When used wisely, an 8 approach can result in the same kind of positive benefits associated with the 8 Destiny Number. Used unwisely, an individual or a city runs the risk of suffering from corruption and all the negative consequences that come with it. (Unfortuantely, the word "corrupt" in regard to various influential Savannah figures, from law enforcement and transportation officials to church leaders and business people, has appeared in quite a few headlines during the past decade.)

The revised Destiny Number for Savannah, taking into account the numbers associated with both the city and state's name, is not 8 but 7. The number 7 is recognized almost universally as one indicating a person of exceptional good fortune, intellectual ability, and spiritual wisdom. Where a city is concerned, it should indicate a locale where education is a noted priority and institutions exist which strongly support learning initiatives. Savannah is in fact home to a number of renowned colleges and universities, including: Savannah State University, Armstrong Atlantic University, Savannah College of Art and Design, Savannah Technical College, and South University Savannah. These and other education outlets serve their intended basic functions but how much they contribute to making the city an intellectual center of any national or international standing is highly debatable. Intellectual achievements are rarely acknowledged in local media while sports and entertainment events receive extended prime-time coverage. The most glaring example of such an instance may be the lack of any electronic media's coverage of author James Alan McPherson's death in 2016. Noting McPherson's long-time "exile" from the city, columnist Bill Dawers stated, "McPherson might have moved on, but it seems like a city that so honors its past would find ways to keep his story—and his stories—alive" (*Savannah Morning News*, "City Talk: Savannah Left Its Mark on James Alan McPherson," July 30, 2016)

An atmosphere of anti-intellectualism is strong enough to have created a steady brain-drain on natives and transients who graduate from area colleges and often afterwards make their way elsewhere as soon as possible. On the other hand, the sheer number of churches seen throughout the Historic District and surrounding wards (or neighborhoods), along synagogues and mosques in the city promote a powerful sense of abiding spirituality also indicative of a 7 Destiny Number. The problem with the number in the destiny position is that it demands the acquisition of different kinds of knowledge for the purposes of establishing greater social harmony in the present and securing beneficial advancements for the future. The city's large number of monuments dedicated to white historical figures compared to the absence of monuments acknowledging individual African-American figures in a town that has always had a large black population is curious indeed. It implies: either attempts to suppress knowledge rather than promote awareness, or a failure to recognize its value and significance. The latter possibility is likely a major contributing factor to the troublesome crime rates.

Pathways and Trends

Many students of numerology consider the Birthpath Number, referred to by some as the Life Path Number, derived from the sum of numbers in a birthdate, to be the most important in a numerological analysis. As master numerologist Matthew Oliver Goodwin put it in his classic text, *Numerology The Complete Guide Volume 1*, for an individual the number represents: "the major lesson to be learned in this life, the central focus of a person's existence... It [also] describes the opportunities available in order to learn the major lesson..."

In addition, the number is considered one of the most reliable because unlike the spelling of a name, birhdates, or founding dates when it comes to places, are less subject to error or change. So what does such a number suggest in reference to a city as opposed to an individual? It spells out the major themes likely to compose the city's history and construct its destiny. Where Savannah is concerned, the Birthpath Number is both exceptional and appropriate because the founding date is February 12, 1733, which reduces to the same as figured as city's Personality Number, which is: 1.

The identical Birthpath and Personality numbers in this case stand as meaningful because as one of the original colonies, Savannah was the first city in Georgia and stands as the oldest. It is also exceptional because 1 is a number which generates new beginnings and independence. Consequently, it urges either a complete break with the past or a view of it that avoids obsession or dependence to the exclusion of blocking different forms of collective advancement. Strength and growth under this numerological vibration comes from cultivating new enterprises, expanding beneficial old ones, and actively seeking untapped opportunities and resources. That creates a sticky situation for a place where large sums of money are generated by showcasing and selling history. The trick, as people in other historic locations like Boston, Philadelphia, Seattle, and New York have learned, is to avoid doing it at the expense of healthy progressive change.

The Obama Connection

It just so happens that the name Barack Hussein Obama and the numeroscope for Savannah Georgia have the number 1 in common. As noted above, the city has the number for both its Personality Number and its Birth Path Number. For Mr. Obama, America's forty-fourth president, it is his Destiny Number. An examination of how the characteristics of the 1 Destiny Number played out during the president's two terms can provide some important lessons when studying how he diplomatically used different functions of his office to correct racial imbalances while simultaneously working on behalf of all Americans. Along these lines, he very successfully used his position to not only appoint highly-qualified and effective African Africans to influential posts, but shined a spotlight on individuals and issues by using such occasions as the Kennedy Center Honors, funeral eulogies (as with Senator Clementa Pinckney's in 2015 and that of the five policemen killed in Dallas in 2016), and presentations of the Presidential Medal of Freedom Award to raise consciousness and rectify problems.

Mr. Obama did not shy away from defending the concerns of the Black Lives Matter movement and, working with Attorney General Eric Holder, began the process of dismantling provisions of the "War on Drugs" that unfairly targeted black men and women. The central objective was never about discriminating in favor of one group or another. It was always about paving a smoother road to justice and equality for a diverse population by doing as much as possible to take racial oppression out of the picture.

Fear of Consequences

Several other numbers are also worth considering in order to understand Savannah from a numerological perspective. For example, its position as the thirteenth colony raises questions about death and rebirth. Can it let go of old definitions and symbols of itself for the sake of embracing new revitalizing ones? That aspect places into an even more interesting perspective the question of why administrators at the state level have been so reluctant to take any tangible action to change the name of Savannah's Eugene Talmadge Memorial Bridge to one that does not glorify white supremacy.

Real change sometimes means letting go of conditions recognized as unjust but which have proven advantageous to a particular group. Upon Donald Trump's election to the U.S. presidency, for example, Nobel Prize for Literature winner Toni Morrison wrote about why a bid to maintain white dominance (in the form of Mr. Trump) had prevailed over experience and knowledge (in the form of Secretary of State Hillary Clinton):

"So scary are the consequences of a collapse of white privilege that many Americans have flocked to a political platform that supports and translates violence against the defenseless as strength. These people are not so much angry as terrified, with the kind of terror that makes knees tremble... On Election Day, how eagerly so many white voters—both the poorly educated and the well educated— embraced the shame and fear sowed by Donald Trump..." (Morrison, New Yorker, "Making America White Again, Nov 21, 2016).

Given Savannah's predominantly black population, it is difficult to understand the example of a bridge bearing an avowed white supremacist's name. Why would such a population not aggressively advocate for a progressive change? Or is the issue regarding it more a matter of a lack of selective awareness, otherwise known as living in a state of denial? Whatever the case may be, the issue of leadership within the city is likely to remain a major one until factors revolving around it are openly addressed and resolved. This is possibly more true for the city's African Americans in leadership positions than for White Americans in leadership positions simply because aggressively addressing racial disparities can make black leaders appear to be biased, whereas doing the same makes white leaders appear liberal or fair-minded. This scenario can hold true for any city, state, or national leader who happens to be black.

The Word 'Potential'

Like psychology or philosophy, numerology is one method of organizing individual perceptions about the world and of framing possible outcomes. With or without its intriguing analytics, Savannah's story as it unfolds continues to be a fascinating one. Potential is a word that has been applicable to the area ever since James Oglethorpe chose to dock at Yamacraw Bluff and subsequently laid out the plans for the city's construction and development, square by square and ward by ward.

In these early 21st century times, the economic prospects presented by its renowned seaport, and its growing reputation as a favorite tourism/vacation destination and filming location, makes the word potential even more significant. One of the central factors surrounding how that potential will be realized revolves largely around how openly and honestly citizens choose to confront issues like race and racism, poverty and classism, education and predatory gentrification. When looking at these subjects in-depth, a person can easily draw the conclusion that although slavery officially ended in the city in 1865 the same as in the rest of America, it would appear that certain patterns of behavior associated with it did not. True freedom, like that of the right to determine one's options and define and claim one's responsibilities, for too many has yet to be established. The work accomplishing it is set in place before they are born.

Appendices

Appendix A:

2016 Statement by Aberjhani

on the Eugene Talmadge Memorial Bridge

Placing Eugene Talmadge's name on the bridge was a very unfortunate mistake that residents of Savannah, Georgia, have the power to correct. I believe it is incumbent upon those people who consider themselves leaders in the city—be they elected officials, educators, ministers, poets, parents, or entertainment celebrities—to help residents and government administrators understand the full implications of not exercising that corrective power.

As it stands, the name makes the bridge nothing less than an official endorsement of the doctrine of white supremacy strategically advocated by former Gov. Eugene Talmadge to win elections, and which his son Sen. Herman Talmadge endorsed in a slightly more covert manner. There are those who may say father and son's collective mindset simply reflected the apartheid Jim Crow times. So be it. Hopefully that insight will inspire them to let their own collective mindset reflect the more progressive practices of these changing 21st-century times.

It should not be necessary in 2016 to stage marches across the bridge or have sit-ins on it to disrupt the illusion, or delusion, of normalcy in order to bring about a crucial intelligent change. There is a big difference between maintaining a Confederate statue that marks an authentic historic site of the Civil War in a popular park and declaring a major public thoroughfare, and landmark, as a memorial to someone who openly advocated racial oppression. We cannot sustain that kind of homage to America's historic brand of an apartheid system and believe it has no impact on the racial and economic inequities Savannah is facing right now.

Yes, the often-reported violence committed against our lives with guns does indeed maim and destroy bodies. But there is also the rarely-reported violence committed against our lives with the outdated policies and prejudices that cripple our souls. We cannot, on the one hand, celebrate the racism of yesteryear and then on the other scratch our heads claiming confusion over the absence of black-owned businesses on Broughton Street, or over the higher-than-national-average level of poverty in the city.

The generation growing into maturity at this moment and those to come deserve a much better legacy than that and it is possible to give them one. Savannah is no longer just a southern city in the antebellum sense of that term. It is a municipality rapidly developing into an expansive center of cosmopolitan distinction. And, possibly more than anything else, it is a beloved hometown that the world should recognize more readily for its fusions of cultural splendor than for the preservation of any slyly-cultivated forms of racism whatsoever.

Aberjhani

©11 April 2016

Appendix B:

2017 Statement by Aberjhani in Response to:

"Re-naming the Talmadge Bridge: A Conversation

About Community Reconciliation and Progress"

The fact that Eugene Talmadge has earned his place in Georgia's and America's history cannot be contested with any seriousness. Whether the history he made—when considering much of it is characterized by his promotion of white supremacy—should be commemorated by maintaining his name on the bridge spanning the Savannah River from the city's downtown area to Hutchinson Island make for a very different discussion.

During the 1930s and 1940s, Mr. Talmadge was not only a true representative of those he considered his constituents. He was also symbolic of White Southern culture in general, and of the heinous Jim Crow apartheid system which legally and socially defined race relations throughout our country during his time. In many ways, Governor Talmadge was a hero to numerous people (just as many currently consider President Donald Trump heroic while others use very different words to describe him). But the governor was certainly not a hero to folks who were, and are, black like me.

In this present moment, people all over the world tend to recognize organizations, structures, products, and even religious institutions by their particular brand: B-R-A-N-D. How a product, or a city—like our beloved Savannah—is branded often determines how people perceive its values, beliefs, operational principles, and perhaps most importantly—its intended function. So let's be very clear about one dominant theme of the Eugene Talmadge brand: he won his elections by making xenophobic pronouncement's warning White constituents they had better vote for him or else Blacks were going to invade their lives in all kinds of unspeakable ways. For that reason: he basically endorsed the practices of domestic terrorism commonly referred to as lynching, forced disenfranchisement, and economic disempowerment directed against African Americans.

The question now is how should we interpret the Talmadge brand of racial demagoguery in *This Year of Our Lord 2017* within a local, national, and international context?

Locally: It is a grievous lingering insult to the indigenous Black population of Savannah, and to Whites who do not count themselves among those aspiring to practice oppression in any form: be it racial, gender-based, economic, religious, or otherwise. Consideration must also be given to the uncomfortable irony of the possibility that Georgia would not exist if James Oglethorpe had responded to Chief Tomochichi the way Mr. Talmadge did toward African Americans. Or, for that matter, if Chief Tomochichi had been a leader more devoted to conflict than diplomacy.

And the truth is that whether we are talking locally, nationally, or globally, retaining the governor's name on the bridge is a betrayal of everything America tells the rest of the world it stands for: things like equal opportunities, social justice, coexistence, and human rights. It is also a betrayal of the word "legacy": as in what we are consciously choosing in this hour to pass on to the current Millennial generation and those who will come after them.

This precise historical moment demands we ask ourselves: do we really want to continue kicking this particular grenade down the road until it blows up in all of our faces? Because make no mistake about it: others are observing and assessing the situation with calculated interest. Without exercising responsibility on our own behalf, it is only a matter of time before more militant elements attempt to exploit the issue to their chaotic advantage.

Lastly: I am going to close out by citing two quotes attributed to Eugene Talmadge and taken from author George Anderson's 1975 book,

The Wild Man from Sugar Creek: the Political Career of Eugene Talmadge. The first is: "If I get a Negro vote it will be an accident" (p. 230). And the second reads: "We are going to flash to the world the news [on September 10, 1942] that Georgia recognizes white supremacy and is a white man's state."(Spoken at a campaign rally in Claxton, reported in *Augusta Chronicle*).

In regard to the first quote—"If I get a Negro vote it will be an accident."—every single African American in the state of Georgia needs to recognize that by not advocating for the removal of Talmadge's name from the bridge, you are in effect voting for a platform dedicated to racial oppression—not racial bias, just straight-up old-fashioned die-hard racism as practiced decades ago by a former governor and still represented by his name today.

Looking at the second quotation— "We are going to flash to the world the news [on September 10, 1942] that Georgia recognizes white supremacy and is a white man's state." That is, in fact, exactly what Talmadge's name broadcasts about Savannah and Georgia to the international crews of those giant container ships that pull into our amazing port. That is what his name announces to the millions of visitors to my hometown every year. It very loudly sends the message that within this city the displacement of indigenous African Americans and the erasure of the history of Georgia's oldest Black community via gentrification or other means—does not matter.

By allowing that profane proclamation to continue transmitting, the Black, White, Asian, Latino, Indian and other diverse residents of Savannah are helping to sustain a toxic culture of regressive repressive racism which should have been reformed in the twentieth century. If you did not realize that before, then hopefully you do now and we can choose in this decisive hour to take meaningful corrective action.

Aberjhani

Sept 2017

Appendix C:

Savannah Community Marks 100th Anniversary

of a Legacy of Knowledge

Community leaders, patrons of the arts, and enthusiastic readers gathered at the historic Carnegie Branch Library in Savannah, Georgia, on November 13, 2014, to commemorate with a new historical marker the legacy established by its African-American founders in 1914.

Among those assembled on the lawn beside the majestic front steps of the library, located at 537 East Henry Street, were: Senator Lester G. Jackson (D-Savannah and Chatham County), cultural arts advocate Dessie Baker, librarian Mark Darby, author and composer Ja A. Jahannes, historian Charles Lwanga Hoskins, Library Board of Trustees Chairman Dr. Daniel Brantley, Georgia Historical Society Executive Director Todd Groce, founder descendant Ursuline Dickey, Dixon Park Neighborhood representative Helen Washington, Library Foundation Director Lester B. Johnson III, Dixon Park Neighborhood representative Helen Washington, Library Foundation Director Lester B. Johnson III, the library's current branch manager Adriene Tillman, and many others.

In his remarks on the historical significance of the library, Sen. Jackson noted that one of the reasons his father first moved their family many years ago from Statesboro to Savannah was to gain access to the library. They settled in a house only two blocks away: "He said son, this neighborhood will be an investment in your future. It has a library… Every Saturday morning before I could go out to play, I had to visit this structure…"

Sen. Jackson added the following:

"A hundred years ago, 11 men got together and invested in this community's future by gathering books. And that's what this marker here stands for today, an investment those men made in the future of not only young people but everyone. It gave them access to knowledge, it gave them access to history, but most importantly it gave them access to the world… where they could come read books, where they could come collect books, where they could come to understand what was [happening] in the world. And that knowledge is still needed today."

The men to whom he was referring established themselves in 1906 as the Colored Library Association of Savannah. With a grant from American industrialist Andrew Carnegie, the group was able to build the unique facility at a cost of $104,041.78 but drew on its own resources and community support to provide operational funds and actual books. Construction of the facility, which stands as the only recognized example of Prairie Style architecture (generally associated with Frank Lloyd Wright) in Savannah, got underway in early 1914. Dedication observances were held for it in August of the same year and construction was completed in 1915.

Harlem Renaissance Connections

The date of the library's construction and opening is particularly significant in light of the Harlem Renaissance that would get underway just as World War I drew to a close. Placed in that context, members of the Colored Library Association of Savannah may be rightly viewed as southern counterparts to such historians and bibliophiles as "the father of black history" Carter G. Woodson and scholar Arthur Schomburg. Like New York's famed Schomburg Center for Black Culture, the Carnegie Branch Library is an exceptional repository of works related to African-American history and culture on local, state, and national levels.

In more recent times, structural damage forced the library to close in 1997. It reopened in August 2004 with a slate of programs that included a lecture and book signing based on Facts on File's *Encyclopedia of the Harlem Renaissance*. In addition to modern technology resources, the renovated library also featured a new east wing dedicated to U.S. Supreme Court Justice Clarence Thomas. The text of the new historical marker notes the significance of its role in the intellectual development of both Justice Thomas and Pulitzer Prize-winning author James Alan McPherson.

To learn more about the Carnegie Branch Library's history, it hours or operation, or current programs please call (912) 651-1973 or visit the Live Oaks Public Libraries website.

by Aberjhani

First published by AXS Entertainment at Examiner.com.

Appendix D: A Legacy Less Traveled

Tourists and new residents make their way to Savannah for a variety of reasons. For anthropologist and museum consultant Dr. Deborah L. Mack, the lure was somewhat different:

"I moved to Savannah because it's the closest thing to Dakar on this side of the Atlantic," she says.

Lest the name Dakar conjure images of a mythological "dark continent," note that the African city of two million is the capital of the Republic of Senegal and was once known as "the Paris of West Africa."

Savannah and Dakar do share important similarities. Both are port cities on the Atlantic coast. Both are rich in history, contain strong cultural diversity, and have comparable ecological environments.

"For an anthropologist," says Mack, "Savannah is a mother lode. The architecture, the food, the air, the weather, the topography of this place is extraordinary. I'm an Africanist, and like I said, this is the closest I can get to it in this country."

The Chicago native and Northwestern University grad has coordinated a number of influential and sometimes groundbreaking exhibits, including for Cincinnati's National Underground Railroad Freedom Center and New York's Schomburg Center for Research in Black Culture.

She was appointed in 2005 to the Scholarly Advisory Committee for the Smithsonian Institute's planned National Museum of African-American History and Culture in Washington, D.C. To place in context how big a deal that is, consider that other committee and council members include famed educator John Hope Franklin, multimedia entrepreneur Quincy Jones, and media powerhouse Oprah Winfrey.

Since moving to Savannah three years ago, Mack has served as a consultant for projects involving Ossabaw Island, the Beach Institute, and the Owens-Thomas House. Recently, however, her work took her into Mississippi blues territory. There, she lent her skills for historical interpretation to the B.B. King Museum and Delta Interpretive Center, scheduled to open in 2007.

"In the tradition of B.B. King's community at the time, the people who were in the neighborhood became his family," she says. "We understood that there was something that B.B. King came from, and that we were obliged to put it out there."

Likewise, when examining Savannah's rich history as promoted by the heritage-tourism industry, Mack saw there was much more to the city's story than is generally discussed — possibly because much of it still remains undocumented.

Because studies of slavery and even life among free African Americans during the 1700s and 1800s focus primarily on rural areas, the public knows relatively little about those African-Americans who lived in urban centers like Savannah. Yet their impact is everywhere, from the buildings in which people reside and work to the foods that literally provide Savannah with much of its cultural flavor.

In addition to the common image of African Americans as domestic servants, they worked in carpentry, masonry, ironwork, gardening, blacksmithing, and other occupations that created the city's physical structures.

A simple example of the unacknowledged African influence on the Historic District was the use of the building material known as "tabby," a mixture of oyster shells, water, and lime in various constructions. Signs on historical sites, such as downtown's Owens-Thomas House, acknowledge that tabby was used in the construction of certain buildings but at present neglect to mention that the word and the formula derive from West African cultures.

To help bring greater balance to the story of Savannah's past as the world knows it, Mack worked with the Telfair Museum of Art to obtain a series of grants from the National Endowment for the Humanities to fund a reinterpretation project for the Owens-Thomas House.

"This reinterpretation will include all the people who lived at this site, the free and enslaved, white and black people. Our hope is to really show all of those who lived here in a three dimensional fashion," says Tania Sammons, curator of the Owens-Thomas House.

"We really want to bring to life all the people who were here, not just the wealthy white men who lived here but their wives, their children, their slaves, and the free African-Americans who interacted with this house."

This closer examination of the Owens-Thomas House will provide more information about the character of its neighborhood. The house contains, after all, one of the very few remaining urban slave quarters in the U.S. and receives some 50,000 visitors every year. What we continue to learn about and from it sheds revealing light on the lives of the African-Americans, enslaved and free, that lived in Savannah from 1750 to 1864.

That knowledge in turn increases our understanding about the realities of slavery, black society (in which some blacks themselves owned slaves) and race relations. Beyond its extraordinary historical value, the reinterpretation project could also boost tourism in the city.

As a tourist destination, Georgia is the third most popular state in the South — behind Florida and North Carolina — and the seventh most popular in the country. Within the state of Georgia, Atlanta reigns at the top. Of the millions who visit Savannah, relatively few are African-American.

The added incentive of a more complete history of the city would likely draw more visitors of every background. However, it is especially likely to draw more African-Americans, a group that spends more than $5 billion annually on leisure travel.

"African-Americans are interested in their historical past and they want to see evidence of it," says Mack. At present, she adds, "it's not so much what there is. It's what there is not. It's what is not said, the great silences that people are suspect of."

Anyone who doubts that need only consider that a group of well-known African-American women authors — including Beverly Jenkins, Evelyn Palfrey and Janice Sims — are touring Savannah this month for an event called "Diva Daze 2006." Members hope to combine work with pleasure, getting a first-hand look at a city some of them may use as a setting for a future novel while also enjoying a birthday celebration.

"The evidence shows that expanding the interpretation, not only here but in other places, allows more people to better connect with this experience," says Mack, "to connect with Savannah's past and feel that they are a part of it — feel that there are parts of it they can relate to."

The treasure of information yet to be unearthed in the Savannah area is vast enough that Mack feels learning to properly perform such work is something natives of the city can and should become more involved in professionally. She notes that the history and culture here is one that has influenced cultures and trends worldwide, yet its value seems to be rarely recognized by those who actually live it.

"We have to put in the hard work, and the discipline, and the professionalism, and the follow through in order to control our stories," she says. "And to have the outcome that we want. It means telling the truth! But it means that the benefits come back into the community as well."

Although the Beach Institute is not currently involved in a reinterpretation project, Mack notes that its current focus on contemporary art shows and other modern cultural events overlooks the facility's original purpose.

Built in 1867, the Beach Institute was originally designed to educate newly-emancipated slaves and help them make the transition to freedom. It continued to serve as an educational facility until 1970.

It could still, Mack believes, serve a more socially and politically functional purpose than it presently does by identifying community needs and fulfilling them. It could also benefit financially by more aggressively documenting and promoting its history.

As for the Owens-Thomas House, the final phase of its reinterpretation project requires sharing with the public whatever new discoveries are made about it.

"I think that within five years we'll see a very different kind of interpretation of historic Savannah than one presently sees," said Mack.

"Because that information is accessible, it will be taught to tour guides in the city. It will be taught to school children. And that expanded approach will really much more realistically show the Savannah of the past, including the domestic, political, commercial, industrial — in all kinds of ways."

Aberjhani

First published in *Connect Savannah Weekly News Magazine* May 10, 2006

Appendix E:

A Place Called Hitch Village and

the Federal Economic Stimulus Package

Formerly a home to more than 300 families, Robert M. Hitch Village was the largest government housing project in Savannah, Georgia, and just happened to be the place where this particular author grew up until the age of twelve. Growing up there as a black youth in the 1960s, I never imagined that one day an African-American president, several years younger than me, would provide the economic push that would make it possible for local leaders to schedule the demolition and reconstruction of my old neighborhood. Just as I had never imagined a day could ever come when such a course of action would prove necessary. Nevertheless, more than half the project's 337 units were unoccupied in late 2008 and boarded windows became a traumatic sight for both lingering and past residents.

While a number of President Barack Obama's critics like to claim he is more showmanship than action, the residents of Hitch Village had to beg to differ as they prepared in 2009 for a temporary exodus that would demonstrate the hardcore reality behind the idea of "change" booming from one American city to another. Of the $787 billion committed to the American Recovery and Reinvestment Act, some $5.3 million was pinched off for the Housing Authority of Savannah; and out of that, $2 million set aside to demolish and then resurrect my boyhood home.

In the poem *Return to Savannah*, the narrator describes himself as:

"...a stupid little Hitch Village boy

feet covered with red dirt

and blackberry stains,

snot flowing like panic and river water…"

What follows is the only known attempted history of the community's exceptional past and its now promising future.

II.

My community, Robert M. Hitch Village—known simply as Hitch Village or "The Village" to those who lived there—was built during the early 1950s and started welcoming poverty-stricken families like mine into its concrete bosom in 1955. It was comprised of courts containing long rectangular apartment blocks. These courts were named after biblical figures like Paul, Cain, Ham, and Ruth. Nestled toward its center were two churches: the Central Missionary Baptist Church on Hitch Drive; and the Second Ebenezer Baptist Church on the Corner of McAllister and Colbert Streets.

Before becoming the model government project it was at the time, the area was something very different known as the Old Fort. Located in the northeast section of the city, the Old Fort was a segregated community in which Whites lived in one section and Blacks in the other. Most, regardless of color, lived in bare-wood single-story frame houses lined along the sides of lanes. Most, regardless of color, were poor.

Drums and Shadows, a book published in 1940 by the Georgia Writers' Project and the University of Georgia, provides revealing insight into the spiritual, economic, and social practices of the black people living in the Old Fort. It was a place in an era when African Americans still frequently referred to grandparents, and even parents, who had actually been slaves. It was also a place where the black residents commonly practiced the kind of Hoodoo magic and conjuring described in Zora Neale Hurston's classic of black folklore and anthropology, *Mules and Men.*

They not only very much believed, back in those days, in the prophetic powers of dreams but lived by them. They took guard against the malicious wizardry of witches said to steal one's youth to restore their own, and they studied with care the healing properties of sacred herbs. At the same time, many also lent support to the charismatic spiritual leader known as Father Divine of the Peace Mission Ministry and practiced industriousness as a way of life. They often grew their own food, made their own clothes, got drunk and fought on Saturday nights, got sober and went to church on Sunday mornings. Some might describe the Old Fort as close to "primitive" but the community was, in fact, one that gave Savannah such exceptional citizens as the future civil rights leader and president of Savannah State College, Prince Jackson, and the gifted jazz pianist James Willis.

Although the physical make-up of the Old Fort evolved dramatically with the establishment of Robert M. Hitch Village, many of the old folk beliefs and practices lingered on. So did the separation of the races, with the economically challenged Whites who had lived in the Old Fort resettling in a second project called Fred Wessels located adjacent to Hitch Village, literally just across Randolph Street, which marked Hitch Village's western boundary. It may have been while walking through Fred Wessels to reach the grocery store or downtown shops on the opposite side of the project that I perfected the practice of keeping my head down to avoid the stare of certain poor Whites who seemed to need little provocation to yell threats, throw stones, or aim guns.

The first time, however, someone felt it necessary to call me "nigger" was when I made the mistake of journeying beyond both Hitch Village and Fred Wessels to get a haircut. I was about eight years old and my mother had sent me with my nephew Kenneth, who could not have been more than four, to the barber shop. For some reason, the shop on Wheaton Street, on the southern border of Hitch Village, was closed that day. Why we were not with one of my older brothers I don't recall, but black children of that time and place rarely stayed children for very long and it may be that this was one of my first outings to indicate that I was growing into a "big boy" whose turn it now was to look after others rather than expect others to look after me. It was something I would do throughout my adolescence and again, later, as an adult offspring.

by Aberjhani

from *The American Poet Who Went Home Again*

9 789388 125956